THE BEST BASH BOOK

it's a God thing!

Other books in the Young Women of Faith Library

The Lily Series
> *Here's Lily*
> *Lily Robbins, M.D. (Medical Dabbler)*
> *Lily and the Creep*
> *Lily's Ultimate Party*

Non-fiction
> *The Beauty Book*
> *The Body Book*
> *The Buddy Book*
> *Dear Diary: A Girl's Book of Devotions*
> *Girlz Want to Know: Answers to Real-Life Questions*

We want to hear from you. Please send your comments about this
book to us in care of the address below. Thank you.

Grand Rapids, MI 49530
www.zonderkidz.com

Young Women of Faith

THE BEST BASH BOOK

it's a God thing!

Written by Nancy Rue
Illustrated by Lyn Boyer

Zonderkidz

Zonder**kidz**™

The children's group of Zondervan

The Best Bash Book
Copyright © 2001 by Women of Faith

Illustrations copyright © 2001 by Lyn Boyer

Requests for information should be addressed to:
Zonderkidz, *Grand Rapids, Michigan 49530*
www.zonderkidz.com

ISBN: 0-310-70065-5

Zonderkidz is a trademark of Zondervan.

Published in association with the literary agency of Alive Communications, Inc., 7680 Goddard Street, Suite 200, Colorado Springs, CO 80920.

Art direction and interior design by Michelle Lenger

Printed in the United States of America

01 02 03 04 05 /❖ DC/ 12 11 10 9 8 7 6 5 4 3

Contents

Let's Par-Tee!

"Let's have a feast and celebrate."
Luke 15:23

It comes to you like a whisper in your ear—the idea to have a party. But once it gets in your head, you can hardly think about anything else, right? While you're taking a bath, doing your homework, listening to the teacher call out the spelling words, you're gnawing on it—What kind of party do I want? Whom should I invite? What will we eat? And what about games—and prizes—and favors?

Maybe it's so big it turns your mind inside out. Or maybe you figure, what's to worry about? It'll all just—happen.

Either way, you definitely need to read on. Giving a party can be the coolest, but you don't want it to turn out like this one.

What's Wrong with This Picture?

Marcie decided she *had* to have a party for her birthday this year. Last year her mom talked her into just having a family dinner, but she got only one good present, from her mom and dad, and it was all over in an hour and—well, that wasn't going to happen this year.

After she begged and whined and nagged at her mom for two days, her mother finally gave in and said she could invite six people over for a Saturday afternoon party. Jazzed, Marcie went to school the next day, ran up to two girls she'd been dying to be friends with all year, Ashley and Chelsea, and told them to be at her house this Saturday at 2:00 for the biggest blowout any-body had given all year. Rebecca was standing there too, and she asked if she could come. Rebecca wasn't Marcie's favorite person. In fact, she didn't seem to be anybody's favorite person, but Marcie told her sure, because she didn't want to hurt her feelings.

It wasn't until Marcie was in the middle of her math assignment an hour later that she realized she'd filled up half her guest limit and hadn't invited her five closest friends yet. She did a little calculating in the margin and also realized that even if she did invite them and not Rebecca, that would be seven. Oh, well, she'd just tell her mom.

That worked for her until first recess, when three other girls came up to her and said they could make it Saturday. Ashley had invited them. Marcie made tracks to Ashley, who said if those three girls weren't invited, then she wasn't going to come. Marcie was now up to ten, and she still had to tell Rebecca she was uninvited. It was no surprise when her mom flipped out when she told her.

"They're all going to have to come if you've invited them," Mom said, "but that means the party is going to have to be a whole lot simpler." Even though Marcie wailed that she'd already told everybody it was going to be the biggest bash anybody had ever thrown, Mom held the line. She had only so much to spend.

Marcie was miserable the whole week. First of all, Ashley and Chelsea's mothers both had other plans for them and wouldn't change because Marcie's party was on such short notice. Then Mom bought the food for the party and "only so much to spend" barely covered some sodas, chips, and a long submarine sandwich each girl would get a piece of. When Marcie started whining about party favors and prizes, Mom almost canceled the whole thing.

But at school, Marcie kept telling the girls it was going to be a blast, and they were so excited that was all they could talk about on the playground or in the cafeteria. Marcie could hardly sleep at night worrying about it, but all she could come up with to make the party the cool bash she'd promised were some lame decorations she made out of whatever she could find in the basement and the idea of going on a scavenger hunt. She had that all planned when she told Mom, who said it was way too dangerous. But Mom did feel sorry for her and said she would make cookies for all the girls to decorate however they wanted to. That was going to have to do for entertainment.

When Saturday came, Marcie wished she'd never had the idea of giving a party in the first place. Her two little sisters wrecked her decorations, which weren't much to begin with. Marcie decided at the last minute to have everybody bring an apron for the cookie decorating, but when she called, two of the girls didn't have one and two others said it sounded dumb and maybe they wouldn't come after all.

By 2:00 Marcie was almost in tears, and it didn't get much better after the guests showed up. They took one look at what was left of her decorations and burst out laughing and couldn't talk about anything else for the first ten minutes. They mostly picked at the long sandwich, and everybody asked for something that wasn't on it. When it was time to open presents, Marcie got things she was sure she'd end up shoving under her bed because most of the girls didn't know her that well and bought things for her that were very un-Marcie.

But the worst part was when they trailed into the kitchen to decorate cookies. Two of the girls sat there and played with the frosting, one got really into it and was upset when there weren't enough sprinkles, and the rest of them got into a food fight and trashed the kitchen.

At 3:15 everybody was ready to go home, and Marcie was ready for them to leave. When the last guest to leave said to her, "I thought this was supposed to be a cool party," Marcie vowed she was never going to throw one again.

So Why Even Bother?

Sounds like parties can be a real pain to give. So why do people have them—all the time?

First of all, parties don't have to be a drag to throw. They're supposed to be fun, for the hostess as well as her guests. But they're fun only if you don't make the mistakes that Marcie did—and Marcie's first big blooper was her reason for giving a party in the first place: it was her birthday and she wanted to make sure she got plenty of "good presents." It also gave her an opportunity to get two "popular" girls to give her some attention. Perfectly reasonable, right?

Wrong!

Birthday parties, like all others, are for celebration. If Marcie had wanted to have a party to celebrate the fact that she was born and to welcome in her new age, her party would have had a better chance of getting off the ground. The whole reason for parties of any kind should be, believe it or not, a God thing.

HOW IS THIS A God Thing?

The Bible is like a party manual! Every time you turn around in there, people are celebrating with music and food and entertainment. They're putting on their best digs and dancing and whooping it up sometimes for days on end. Let's look at some of their reasons for rolling up the carpets and breaking out the balloons and streamers.

Samson, like most bridegrooms, gave a feast to celebrate his marriage (Judges 14:10). It lasted for seven days. Now *that's* a party.

Abraham held a spur-of-the-moment party for unexpected visitors he was glad to see (Genesis 18:1–8).

The father in the parable of the prodigal son threw a major celebration when his son came home ready to clean up his act (Luke 15:22–24). His father killed an entire calf for him—which is a *lot* of hamburgers.

Levi had a banquet for somebody he wanted a lot of other people to meet (Luke 5:29–30). That somebody, of course, was Jesus.

King Saul gave a feast for the New Moon festival (1 Samuel 20:5). Any excuse for a party, right?

And speaking of any excuse, the woman in Jesus' parable put on a bash when she found a coin she'd lost (Luke 15:8–10).

Jesus himself seemed to enjoy a good party. He went to weddings (John 2:1–10) and dinner parties (Luke 7:36–50) and even gave a Passover feast of his own (Mark 14:12–31), complete with foot washing. He knew how much people loved festive get-togethers, so when he was trying to help them understand things about God, he used feasts as examples. "The kingdom of heaven," he told them once, "is like a king who prepared a wedding banquet for his son" (Matthew 22:1–14).

So it looks like a party is a God thing, right? It is when it's given for the right reasons:

- to celebrate one of God's children—maybe a birthday or a big accomplishment like better grades after a long stretch of not-so-hot ones

- to welcome a change that God has brought about—like a move to a new place or the start of a new school year
- to make somebody—or a lot of somebodies—feel special—like when somebody's going on a trip or a team has won its first game
- to recognize a special event—like Christmas or a baptism
- to bring people together in fellowship—like a costume party for your Sunday school class or a block party for the kids in your neighborhood

But we also find out, if we study Bible parties, that sometimes a bash is thrown for reasons that aren't such a God thing. Check these out:

- The Israelites partied big time to celebrate the golden calf they'd made to worship instead of God (Exodus 32:5–6).
- King Belshazzar had a feast to show off the stuff his father had stolen from the temple (Daniel 5:1–6).
- King Xerxes invited everybody in the kingdom to his place for a shindig, just to make sure everybody saw his wealth (Esther 1:2–8).

We could go on to mention King Herod throwing a birthday party for himself so everybody could carry on for days and practically explode with all the junk food they stuffed in. The point is, if your reason for giving a party isn't a God thing, you've already started off on the wrong foot. Look through the list of party reasons below and put a check by only those you think would be okay with God. Would Jesus come to your party if he knew why you were having it? I think you'll be surprised at what you know about this already.

_____You figure the more people you invite to your birthday party, the more presents you'll get.

_____The only girl who gets better grades than you in your class gave a really lame party. You'd like to give one that will outdo her.

_____Your best friend is moving away, and you want to give her a going-away party to make her feel better and show her how much everybody loves her.

_____You're the only one in your class who hasn't given a party yet this year.

_____ A girl you don't like very much is having a sleepover, so you're going to have one on the same night, so that maybe hers will be a flop.

_____ Everybody is all bummed out because it's January and there's nothing to look forward to.

_____ Your family just set up a home theater in the basement, and you want to share it with your friends.

_____ Your family just set up a home theater in the basement, and you want to show it off to kids who have been making fun of you in school.

_____ You want to have an autumn party on October 31 for all your friends whose parents, like yours, don't want them celebrating Halloween.

Are You Ready to Throw a Party?

We've pretty much figured out that Marcie was giving a party for the wrong reasons, but that wasn't the only cause for her birthday bash bombing. Marcie probably wasn't party ready.

Think back to what she did when she got the idea to have a party. First she wheedled at her mom until the poor woman gave in to get Marcie off her back. Since Mom wasn't enthusiastic, she wasn't willing to help Marcie much along the way—and who can blame her? Have you ever given in to your brother or sister over something you didn't want to do? Have you ever enjoyed doing it? Not!

Second, Marcie didn't know the first thing about creating "the biggest blowout anybody had thrown all year," and she didn't bother to find out. If she had, her party would have been, if not the "biggest blowout," then at least a better time for everybody than it was. Marcie wasn't ready, or willing, to make plans, discuss things with her mom, write out a guest list, send invitations, or wait until it was a better time, financially, for her parents to help her out or even earn some bucks herself to buy the decorations, favors, and prizes she dreamed about.

How do you know when you're ready?

✿ *ZOOEY: I really want to have a party, but every time I think about nobody coming, I get all clammy and change my mind. Am I ready?*

I'm sure somebody would come, Zooey, but since you're worried about it, maybe you could spend some time making sure your friendships are in good shape. (Maybe you should read *The Buddy Book*!) Feel good about your close friendships first. Then you won't have to worry about people ditching your party. You'll know you're ready.

✿ *RENI: This party thing sounds like a lot of trouble to me. What if Shad Shifferdecker shows up with his jerky friend just to mess it up? What if the ice cream melts all over or my parents hang around too much? It doesn't sound like it's worth it, but I guess I should have one. I'm ready, aren't I?*

Actually not, Reni. A party is supposed to be fun, not just for your guests but for you too. If your heart isn't in it, don't do it. It's not like doing your homework. You don't have to give one!

✿ *KRESHA: I want to have a party, but we don't have a nice house or a lot of money. I think I would be embarrassed to have a lot of people over. I'm not ready, am I?*

I think you're ready, but the circumstances aren't. Perhaps you could do something else for the people you like besides have a party. You can make some ideas from this book simpler for a few friends. Real friends would never make you feel embarrassed about your own home.

✿ *SUZY: Am I supposed to have a party sometime? I'm so shy—it doesn't sound like that much fun to me.*

Not everybody was born to be a hostess at twelve! Wait a little while until you feel more comfortable with your friends. Meanwhile, you could practice on your own family. Could you have a breakfast-in-bed party for just you and your mom and dad and sisters for Mother's Day or Father's Day? Could you have a mini-slumber party for you and your sisters and maybe one of your friends? You're probably more ready than you think. Just start slowly, and you'll find out how giving a party can help you with your shyness.

❀ *LILY: I have so many ideas for good parties. I'm always dreaming up ways to make invitations and decorations. I haven't given one myself, without my mom doing everything, but I think I could with some help from her. But I'm only twelve. Am I ready?*

It sure sounds like it to me! You've got the party spirit, and heaven knows you have the energy. Read this book and use it to help plan a gig, with your mom's help and permission, of course. You'll do a great job!

CHECK Yourself OUT

Next to each of these statements that sounds like you, draw a little party hat. This will help you find out how ready you are to take the party plunge.

_____ I like to go to parties. I think they're the best!

_____ I think parties are a cool way to cele-brate stuff—better than getting something new or going out to eat.

_____ I can turn just about any occasion into a party. I do things like make popcorn when my family watches a video, decorate my dad's car on his birthday, or make a banner when my baby brother learned to walk.

_____ I like to plan. I'm really into daydreaming or making lists or putting together scrapbooks. I get a picture in my head of how I want things to be.

_____ I don't mind working hard for things. I don't always expect every-body else to do stuff for me.

_____ My parents don't seem to be worrying about money right now.

_____ My parents don't seem to be worrying about *anything* big right now (we're not about to have a new baby, move away, have my grand-mother move in, or stuff like that).

_____ I usually finish what I start.

Now count up your party hats.

If you have 7 or 8 hats, girl, you're a party animal! Not only are you ready to do this thing yourself, but conditions at home are right for party time as well. Since you probably don't have your own place, you will have to get permission and count on your folks for help—and the cash to back your little soirée. (That's French for party. You can knock your friends' socks off with that.) This book can help you plan your get-together and make it something your friends will want to do again. Sharpen your pencil and read on.

If you have 4, 5, or 6 party hats, you're mostly ready, but there are some things you should consider before you approach your mom or dad with the idea. Look at the statements you didn't give hats to. Pay careful attention to those as you read this book. If you can work those out, it's party time!

If you have 1, 2, or 3 party hats, there are probably some things that need to be looked at before you start sending out invitations. Read this book carefully and talk to your mom or dad about the statements you didn't give hats to. When everybody's sure those things have been taken care of, you're ready to make up a guest list. Until then it'll be a fun thing to think and dream about—and what's the fun of being a girl if you can't think and dream?

What Does the Ultimate Bash Look Like?

Before we go on to party planning, let's take a look at an example of what we're planning. There are, of course, a bazillion ways to throw a party, but here's what Marcie's party could have looked like if she'd read *The Best Bash Book*.

Marcie's birthday was coming up, and she decided this year she'd like to have a party with some of her friends, instead of just a family dinner. She was excited about turning twelve, and she wanted to celebrate it with some others who were having the twelve experience too. She had in mind inviting almost every girl in the class over for seven kinds of pizza and a bag full of goodies for each girl to take home, but she figured she'd better ask her mom before she went any further with her plans.

Her mom wasn't thrilled with the idea at first, because, as she explained to Marcie, the family had had some unexpected expenses lately and there wasn't a lot of money for extras. But she told Marcie that if she would be willing to limit the guest list to six, she might be able to finance a nice get-together for Marcie. Marcie was a little disappointed, but she tried to be mature about it. She made up a list of every girl she wanted to have come, but it was about twelve people long. After a lot of thinking and praying, she got it down to six girls she really liked and who really liked her. She had to drop off the two popular girls who got invited to every party, but that was okay because they hardly ever talked to Marcie anyway.

Then she thought about what kind of party she wanted. When she was a kid she always had a theme, like Little Mermaid or Star Wars. This time she wanted something more grown-up. What about a What I Want to Look Like When I Grow Up Party? She could make invitations that looked like mirrors, made with some aluminum foil. Maybe it could be a tea party. Mom liked the idea, and she helped Marcie get started on the invitations. Then Mom suggested they deliver the invitations to the girls' houses instead of having Marcie hand them out at school. That way nobody who wasn't invited would get her feelings hurt when the envelopes showed up in the classroom. Before Marcie started filling in the insides of the mirror cards, they talked about date and time. Tea was usually at 4:00, so that part wasn't hard. But her birthday was this Saturday, and that might be short notice. They decided to make it the next Saturday to give her friends more planning time. Marcie put everything her friends would need to know on the invitations—what to wear, what to bring, and how long the party would last. That way nobody would show up in jeans or think they were supposed to stay for dinner.

Once the invitations were out, Marcie started planning her decorations. She had to keep them simple because of the money factor, but Mom reminded her that grown-up parties didn't usually use balloons and streamers anyway. They decided on an arrangement of flowers in the middle of the table, place cards at each place, and a little spray of flowers tied with a ribbon for each girl to take home.

What were they going to do at this party, Mom wanted to know, besides eat and open presents? The guests could each tell why they dressed the way they did and explain what they wanted to look like when they grew up. Mom said she could ask her friend the beautician to come in and show them how to do their nails or something. And what about one game? It would have to be quiet, since they would be all dressed up. Marcie decided on charades: acting out careers the girls could go into.

Next, Marcie made up a menu and showed it to her mother. Mom was impressed that Marcie didn't go overboard. She wanted pink lemonade instead of tea, although it could still be served in china cups from a teapot. She thought individual cupcakes would be better than a big birthday cake. And sherbet would look pretty in those cool dessert dishes Mom had. Mom suggested a little cup of nuts and mints at each place too.

Marcie was so excited she could hardly wait until next Saturday. She still had a lot to do though. She helped with the shopping, helped find a babysitter who would take her two lit-tle sisters away for the two hours the party was going on, and helped clean the house and set the table and make the cupcakes.

Finally Saturday arrived—and so did the guests. They were all dressed to the max, some of them with hats and gloves. It was so cool to see everybody looking grown up. Everybody who was invited came, and each girl brought Marcie a present she loved. She'd almost forgotten about that part, which made opening them even more fun. The games were well planned, so they went smoothly. Soon everybody was ready to eat. The tea party was so differ-ent it made everybody feel special, particularly when Marcie told them they could take their nuts and mints and flowers home.

When it was 6:00 nobody wanted to leave—but they did because their par-ents knew right when to pick them up. While Marcie shared the leftover cup-cakes with her two little sisters as she told them all about it, their eyes shone like they couldn't wait to be as old as Marcie and throw their own parties.

Just Do It

Just to show yourself that you already know a lot about what it takes to throw an amazing party, draw a balloon next to each statement that tells what Marcie did this second time around to make her tea party all she dreamed it would be. Leave the rest blank.

_____ She wanted the party because everybody else was having one.

_____ She wanted the party because she wanted to celebrate her birthday with her friends.

_____ She checked everything out with her mom first.

_____ She planned the whole thing out herself and told her mom she'd have to pay for it.

_____ She made up the guest list and then found out how many people she could actually have.

_____ She found out how many people she could have and then made up the guest list.

_____ She had a theme and planned everything around that.

_____ She figured a party was a party and people could just make their own fun when they got there.

_____ She picked out food that was different but that she knew they would like.

_____ She picked out the same food everybody has at their parties.

_____ She was really nervous and couldn't have a good time because she was worried about what everybody thought.

_____ She had worked out everything beforehand so she could have a good time herself.

Talking to God About It

Nothing is too small, too unimportant, too "not serious" to talk over with God before you do it. After all, don't we want everything we do to meet God's approval? Why should a party be any different? Take your party concerns to your Best Pal. Use this prayer starter if it helps.

Dear _____, (your favorite way of addressing God)

Wow—I'm old enough to help plan my own parties: not just tell my mom what kind of cake I want—but really do it.

I'm_____ about that, God, and I know you understand.

Would you help me know if I'm really ready? The Check Yourself Out quiz said I might need to look at _____.
Would you guide me to the help I need? Would you help me be patient and wait if I need to?

God, I'd like to have a party because _____. I sure would love it if you would help me make sure that's a good reason.

And most of all, God, please help me to remember that even a party should be all about you in spirit. Don't ever let me stray from that, okay?

I love you, God. I celebrate you.

Amen,

_____ (your name)

Lily Pad

The worst experience I ever had at a party was . . .

Getting There Is Half the Fun

"Where do you want us to make preparations
for you to eat the Passover?"
Matthew 26:17

Why All This Planning?
Why Can't We Just Have a Party?

Remember when you were little and it was time for your birthday? Probably all you did was tell your mom what kind of cake and ice cream you wanted, and she did the rest. Party hats, balloons, and streamers appeared as if placed there by the Party Fairy. Games materialized, and so did the prizes. Somehow, it was all wonderful. Why is it so different now?

Don't think for a minute that your mom didn't make lists and think things through before all those four-year-olds stormed the front door. The only thing that's different now is that *you* can take part in the planning. If you start far enough ahead and have the right attitude, dreaming up a party and making the preparations is almost as much fun as the party itself. Besides, as you've no doubt guessed, planning is a God thing.

HOW IS THIS A God Thing?

Even Jesus, busy as he was with saving the world, took the time to make preparations for the biggest feast of the Jewish year—the Passover. He was getting ready to go into Jerusalem, where he knew he was going to be *crucified,* but he stopped and made his party plans.

Jesus told the disciples to go into the city to a certain man he'd already made arrangements with and tell him Jesus was going to celebrate the Passover with his disciples in this man's guest room on his upper floor. Naturally, they followed his directions and found everything just as he'd said it would be so they could prepare. When the evening came, everything was in order.

- The table was big enough so Jesus and all twelve of the disciples could recline while they ate. (Far cry from your mom telling you to quit slouching!)
- The bowls were filled with enough food for all of them to eat.
- The right kind of bread and the right kind of wine were available—just what Jesus needed

to introduce the symbolic Holy Communion that Christians still celebrate today.

• Jesus had an agenda for the evening: eat, tell them what was about to happen to him, and sing a hymn.

Jesus wanted everything just right for this important event. When you give a party, if your reasons are right, as we chatted about in chapter 1, you'll want everything just so for *your* guests as well, so they'll feel special and remember your get-together for a long time. Even Jesus, with all his power, knew it wasn't just going to happen!

Other Reasons Maybe Jesus Didn't Consider!

- You know what you and your friends like to do and eat, so who but you should get it all ready for your party beforehand? ("Grandma, you gave me great parties when I was in preschool, but I think my friends might laugh if I have a Barney cake. Why don't you let me plan this one, okay?")
- It teaches you how to be a confident hostess, a skill that doesn't hurt to have as you get older. In fact, it helps you learn confidence period. You make plans, you see them turn out, you realize you do make a difference. ("Wow—that was a neat party! If I can plan that, I can probably plan a totally cool science project.")
- If you plan, you'll be able to relax and have a good time at your own party, instead of stressing out at the last minute and wishing you'd never sent out the invitations. ("I wish everybody would go home. I need a nap.")
- If you think things through beforehand, you won't have the kinds of disasters that will make you legendary in school for years to come. ("That's Susy Schmo. Remember that party she gave in fifth grade where nobody liked the licorice cake so everybody ended up throwing it at each other, right in her mom's dining room?")

What Kind of Planner Are You?

If the idea of making decisions and lists makes you want to forget the whole thing, don't panic. Anybody can make a plan. You just have to know what kind of planner you are and go with that. It's time to . . .

CHECK
Yourself OUT

Circle the response that sounds the most like you. Remember, it doesn't have to be exact.

1. When it's time to decide what I want for Christmas, I would rather

   a. write a detailed letter to my parents, with colored ink and stickers and drawings
   b. whip off a quick list on the back of an old homework paper
   c. tell my mom while we're in the car running errands

2. If I had to come up with an idea for a story, I would like to

   a. sit down with a clean pad of paper and a sharpened pencil with a good eraser and wait for an idea
   b. lie on my back in bed and daydream about it until it came to me
   c. talk to somebody—like my best friend or my mom or my sister—and brainstorm for ideas together

3. When I go shopping with my mom, I like it when

   a. she has a list and I know exactly what we're going to buy
   b. we have an idea what we want but we look at all the possibilities when we get there too
   c. we wander around the store until we see something we want or need

4. When I have a big project due at school, it's natural for me to

   a. start working on it as soon as the teacher makes the assignment
   b. take a while to get into it, which I usually do well before it's due
   c. wait until the last possible minute and then really hustle

5. If I decided exactly what color I wanted my room painted, I

   a. wouldn't change my mind about it no matter what
   b. would consider a change if somebody showed me something that really caught my attention

c. would probably change my mind a dozen times before the paint got on the walls, and even then . . .

Okay, count up your a's, b's, and c's and put your numbers in the spaces:

_____ a's   _____ b's   _____ c's

If you had more a's than other letters, you're the kind of planner who loves making lists and likes everything to be on paper. When you make up your mind about something, it probably takes an act of Congress to change it. As you read about party planning here in *The Best Bash Book* and perhaps plan your own ultimate bash, don't be afraid to get right on it, since that's what you love to do. Be sure to have plenty of paper and pencils around, and enjoy writing down every last detail. You're going to love the planning. But remember to be flexible too. You're a great one for planning ahead, but don't miss out on spur-of-the-moment fun as well.

If you had more b's than other letters, you probably have such vivid ideas you don't have to write down what color plastic forks you want. Maybe you like to leave some of the decisions for when you get to the store or when a great idea comes to you as you're falling asleep. That's okay! If you use the Ultimate Party Planning Sheet in the back of this book, you can get yourself a fun marker and simply check off things as you do them. Go ahead and rely on your wonderful, creative self. Do refer to your list once in a while to make sure you're doing what needs to be done—not just dreaming it up!

If you had more c's than other letters, the word *planning* probably gets the same reaction from you as the word *trapezoid*. What's *that?* Actually, you still plan—you're just a little bizarre about it! If you're going to plan a party, you'll want to come up with ideas while you're riding in the car to gymnastics class or brushing your teeth before bed. Then you'll like brainstorming those ideas with anybody who'll listen. It'll be a good idea at that point to have somebody write them down for you—because you'd probably rather have a tooth pulled than write them down yourself! Your party will most likely be a smashing success because you will have considered every possible idea along the way. Just be sure to stop making changes when the food and decorations have been bought, the invitations have been sent out, and the guests are ringing the doorbell! In fact, your biggest challenge will be not to leave everything until the last minute. Get somebody to help you who is willing to nudge you along, and you'll be fine.

Formal Ball or Backyard Picnic?

The absolute first thing you need to do, once you've decided it's time to plan a party, is decide what kind of party it's going to be. Unlike when you were five and one birthday party was pretty much like another, you have choices now, and the possibilities are so endless it boggles the mind.

Here are some things to consider to help you narrow down your options.

Just Do It

What's your style? Your best bet is to choose a party that fits you. If you're comfortable and enthusiastic, your guests will be too. To get a feel for your party style, circle all of the parties below that you would like to go to or even give. Circle only the ones that really appeal to you.

A	B	C
Carnival fun night	Swimming party	Going to a museum party
Fifties party	Hiking party	Mystery party
Hawaiian slumber party	Campout slumber party	Movie night slumber party
Career costume party	Party on the beach	Victorian tea party
Backwards party	Backyard Olympics	Paint your own T-shirt party

If you circled the most parties in the A column, you probably like parties that are really different and have a lot of unusual things to do. As you read *The Best Bash Book*, you'll notice that at the end of each chapter, a certain type of party is featured. Look carefully at The Ultimate Theme Party in chapter 3, The Ultimate Costume Gig in chapter 5, and some of the wild ideas for The Ultimate Sleepover at the end of this chapter. Then let your imagination run wild—within Mom-limits, of course!

If you circled the most parties in the B column, you really like to be outside doing outside stuff. Why not plan a party that happens at the park, the beach, or even your own backyard? If you're happiest when you're outside, take your friends with you! Looking at the special party feature at the end of each chapter, pay especially close attention to The Ultimate Field-Trip Party in chapter 7 and the Camp-In Slumber Party in the Ultimate Sleepover section at the end of this chapter.

If you circled the most parties in the C column, you may have quieter interests, which include learning new things. Those very interests can make great parties, even for your livelier friends. There will be some ideas that will appeal to you in the Ultimate Sleepover section at the end of this chapter, as well as in the Ultimate Costume Gig (chapter 5) and the Ultimate Field-Trip Party (chapter 7).

Every special parties section includes ideas for ultimate parties to fit your own style. Anybody can have an Ultimate Birthday Bash (chapter 4) or Ultimate Boy-Girl Get-Together (chapter 6) as long as she takes her own personality into consideration.

Blockbuster Bash or Mini-Party?

The next thing to consider is the size of your party. Are we talking everybody you know in a room the size of a gymnasium, your three closest friends gathered in your breakfast nook, or something in between? Before you make that decision, keep these things in mind.

- *How much space you have.* Nothing kills a party faster than kids feeling like they're crammed into an elevator. People get cranky because somebody's elbow is in their ice cream. Games flop because there's no room to play them. Stuff gets knocked off walls and shelves—and parents scowl. Consider where your party is going to be and then picture your guests in there. Twenty people may fit in your backyard, but possibly not in your living room.

- *Your reason for giving the party.* If it's to celebrate your birthday, you probably don't want everyone you've ever laid eyes on. That looks like a move to rake in the presents. On the other hand, if it's to introduce a lot of people to the new kid on the block, you'll want to include, well, a lot of people!

- *What kind of party it is.* Sleepovers usually go better with smaller numbers. Costume parties are more fun with lots of people. A party where you're going to choose teams for relays will call for more guests than one where a clown is coming in to put face paint on everybody.
- *Your parents.* Oh, yeah, them—you know, the people who own the house and who are probably going to be paying for your shindig? It's always nice to consider what they are willing to okay. Keep *their* personalities in mind as well as yours when you're dreaming up party ideas. Some dads love to install horseshoe pits or build puppet theaters for their little darlings. Others would rather pile everybody into the minivan and treat you all to a movie and popcorn. If you have your heart set on an elaborate Colonial American tea party and your mom, the tennis-playing football fan, looks like she's going to go into a coma at the idea of teapots and silver spoons, be ready to compromise. Maybe a Mad Hatter tea party would work better for both of you. Moms and dads usually have a budget too, so funds probably won't be unlimited for your ultimate party. How much they have to spend will help determine the scope of your party. It's best not to beg for more. Not only is that bad form, but it also makes parents feel bad. Every mom and dad would love to be able to make their daughter's dreams come true, and it feels crummy when they're reminded—in that same daughter's whiny voice—that they can't.

Besides, bigger doesn't necessarily mean better. It isn't how many people you invite or how big a hall you can rent to house your dream that makes a party the delight you want it to be. It's the love and the creativity and the planning you put into it. No matter what kind of party you give, or what size it is, if you use the Ultimate Party Planning Sheet at the end of the book—and use it according to your own planning style—your bash is going to be the best. Each chapter in *The Best Bash Book* will go into lots of detail about the things on the list, so don't start to fill it in yet. For now, just take a look at the fun that lies ahead. If you're planning a party while you read this book, you can fill it in as you go, or you can go to it any time you're ready to get started.

Right now, let's enjoy the dreaming, the ideas, and the visions. Let it be delicious in your head as you read on!

Talking to God About It

Are there things about planning a party that you'd like to talk to God about? Keeping in mind that nothing is too small or silly or funky to take to our heavenly Father, make a list of the things you'd like to chat with him about when you take quiet time to pray. You may already know what you plan to discuss with him, but this list might help you. Do you want to talk to God about—

- not wanting to go to all the trouble to plan?
- not being able to make decisions about stuff?
- your family scoffing at your style of making plans?
- not having enough money or space for the party you want?
- whether you'll be able to agree with your parents on the party details?
- being able to do all the stuff you promise to do instead of your mom ending up doing it all because you slack off?

Don't forget to thank him for inventing parties in the first place. This is fun stuff!

Lily Pad

If I had all the money and space and parents' approval I needed, boy, the party I would plan.

It would be like this . . .

Special Party Feature: THE ULTIMATE SLEEPOVER

Does the idea of a party where you invite some of your girlfriends over to spend the night send little goose bumps up and down your spine? Give you the giggles just thinking about it? Make you want to break out the sleeping bags right away?

Then you need to give the ultimate sleepover, girl! Here's the deal.

It Looks Like This: Girlfriends get together for an evening of games, a fun dinner and/or snacks, lots of talking and giggling, and a whole night spent either sleeping in sleeping bags or doing more whispering and giggling (also in sleeping bags)! Design a sleepover for your style of party giver.

It Needs This Much Space: You'll need enough room for each girl to roll out her sleeping bag and park her backpack or duffel bag (the one she brings full of pj's, toothbrush, and other sleepover paraphernalia). Your family room or living room might be perfect, but check out with your parents whether they're willing to give up that much of the house for a whole evening and night. Will they be able to keep your little brothers and sisters out of there when their favorite TV show comes on, for instance? You might want to have a separate "You're Actually Going to Sleep?" room for girls who get tired and want to go to sleep while the nocturnal ones stay up and play the night away.

The Guest List: Six or eight girls is a good number for a sleepover. It's good to invite an even number so nobody gets left out. Sleepovers usually go best when everyone already knows each other and everyone hits it off with the others in the group. Remember, a whole night is a long time!

Inviting Ideas: Create invitations that have something to do with spending the night. Could you make paper-doll pajamas and write the party info on the back? Could you make tiny pillows out of fabric and write the invitations on them? What about fun toothbrushes with the invitations tied to them with ribbon? In addition to the usual stuff you put on an invitation (which you'll learn about in the next chapter) be sure to include what food is going to be served (dinner, snacks, and breakfast or only some of those) and what special things you want the girls to bring (sleeping bags, pillows, their baby picture).

Food for Thought: Everybody gets really excited about a sleepover, so sitting down to a huge meal doesn't always go over the best. If you want to have **supper** for your guests, try a whole bunch of finger foods, like mini-pizzas, pizza bagels, pigs in a blanket (you know, hot dogs rolled up in crescent-roll dough and baked), or a big sub sandwich you can cut into pieces. It might be fun to have small pizzas already rolled out with tomato sauce on them and bowls of toppings so your guests can make their own. You can do the same thing with sandwiches, crackers, or even Boboli bread. The eating doesn't usually end with supper, of course. Sleepover guests tend to graze on into the next morning! Your **snack** choices will depend on your party theme—popcorn for a Movie Night, S'mores and trail mix for a camp-in.

Avoid foods that are really messy or that could destroy your mom's carpet if they get dropped on the floor, which they most certainly will. For instance, gummy bears and pretzels are a safer bet than M&Ms and Popsicles. If you are going to do something that's potentially sloppy, like having make-your-own sundaes at midnight, do it in the kitchen where cleanup will be a breeze. Most sleepovers end with **breakfast** before guests stumble off to their homes to sleep all day (which, by the way, makes Friday night the best night for a slumber party). It doesn't have to be a full meal, especially since a lot of people don't like to chow down when they first get up—especially if they've barely closed an eye! Some light, fun morning meals include breakfast sundaes they can make themselves from a variety of yogurt flavors, fruits, cereals, and granola;

frozen waffles they toast and top with peanut butter, jelly, honey, fruit, cream cheese, applesauce—whatever you set out on the breakfast bar; an assortment of muffins, little cereal boxes, fruit, hard-boiled eggs, and juice boxes they can stash in fun bags and take back to their sleeping bags with them (don't forget the napkins for this one)! Of course, if your mom and dad are into making the world's greatest pancakes or waffles or breakfast burritos and they want to serve them to you as you all stagger to the table, that's great too!

Do Me a Favor: It's fun to send sleepover guests home with a memento of the night. Could you get your mom or dad to take a Polaroid pic of each girl before she gets up in the morning? Can you give out awards at breakfast (like best giggler and biggest night owl)? Maybe have a Bible verse to tuck into each girl's bag so she'll find it when she unpacks? Or maybe this would be a good time to hand out fun toothbrushes!

Stuff to Do: There are two kinds of activities you'll need to plan for an all-night girlfriend party. First, think of three big games or craft projects or activities that you'll do before people start to drop off to sleep—say, before eleven. What you do will depend on your party theme, but you will want to avoid games that can get too rowdy (ones that involve throwing things, for instance!) and games that could lead to hurt feelings or be embarrassing (like

truth or dare). Stay away from too much competition too—losing is hard for some people, and you don't want anyone to spend a miserable night. Fun games include musical sleeping bags, a huge checkers game with stuffed animals as checkers, or a scavenger hunt you play using catalogues. At least one craft project is always fun—making masks, decorating big cookies, designing journal covers (homemade blank ones and art supplies provided by you), making jewelry out of fun stuff (like buttons, beads, yarn)—anything where each person can be creative without having to be Leonardo da Vinci. The other kind of activities will be things girls can do whenever they feel like it, especially after the main games are over. If you don't provide those night owls with something to do, they'll get bored, and that's death to a party. So have a number of things each girl needs to do before morning. Here are some ideas: put up a big piece of blank paper that covers a lot of space and provide markers for writing and drawing whatever your guests want to; have a task chart and a basket of fun stuff like yo-yos, jacks, Playdough—each girl has to achieve some assigned task with each toy to get stars on the chart; have everyone autograph the plain white pillowcase you handed out to each guest at the beginning of the party; create a gift using items on the craft bar for the person whose name you pull out of a basket. Get the idea? When most people are starting to wind down from all this action, it's a good idea to plug in a movie or turn out the lights and play some prearranged story games. Remember that nobody has to stay up all night (and no "punishments" for girls who don't, like panties put in the freezer, etc.!), and make it okay for guests to drift off during a quiet activity.

Dressing It Up: Since a lot of people don't decorate for a sleepover, you can surprise your friends with something special. Again, it depends on your party theme, but if your approach is simply Traditional Sleepover, think about these ideas. Make a huge tent in your party room with paper streamers or strips of Mylar—that long, shiny stuff that's kind of like big tinsel. It comes in lengths like a hula skirt. Put up twinkle lights so the room will have a special glow even after the main lights are out. Set up a place for kicking back, like a pile of pillows, some beanbag chairs, and a few giant stuffed animals. Go all out to make the party room a really cool place to be, where it's fun and cozy and girls will want to celebrate being friends all night long.

Caution: A sleepover can either be something you'll never forget or the worst night of your life! If you're careful about these things, it *will* be an event you'll want in your scrapbook.

- Check out everything you're planning to do with your mom and dad. No secrets and surprises!
- Be sure your friends know—either you or your parents tell them— what the rules are.
- Check ahead of time to make sure no one has food allergies. If some- one does, have your mom talk to that guest's mom.
- Put a night-light in the bathroom and in the hall that leads to it.
- Nip gossip in the bud.
- At the first sign that somebody wants to stray from the planned agenda or the rules—wants to call boys, suggests you all see if you can sneak out the window, says "Let's put shaving cream in Annie's hand while she's sleeping," that kind of thing—calmly and firmly say no. If she insists, grab your mom. A lot of other people at your party will be glad you did.

You're Invited to a Party!

"At the time of the banquet he sent his servant to tell those who had been invited, 'Come, for everything is now ready.'"

Luke 14:17

Just a Hundred of My Closest Friends ...

We talked in chapter 2 about how *many* people to invite to a party. Remember that it depends on what kind of party it is, how big your space is, and what your parents will allow.

Once you have that determined, it's time to decide who goes on that guest list. You just write down the names of your friends, right?

Uh, no. It's harder than it sounds.

What if you have more friends than you are allowed to invite and you know somebody's going to have hurt feelings?

What if you have two groups of friends and one group isn't crazy about the other one?

What if you have one friend you do fine with when it's just the two of you, but she gets bossy and possessive when there's a crowd?

What if there's somebody your mom says you have to invite—and you'd rather have your head shaved than do it?

Looks like we better ask God about this one.

HOW IS THIS A God Thing?

If you read about all the feasts and banquets in the Bible—and there are a lot of them because those Bible folks loved to party!—you'll find that every one of them was designed to celebrate something. The ones God blessed, of course, were the ones that celebrated him in some way—like marriages and funerals and birthdays and grape gatherings and sheep shearings. Sometimes the party givers spent weeks preparing the food, because they wanted every detail to be perfect for God.

That would include the guest list, then, yeah? Yeah! But don't panic. God has some pretty good guidelines for you on that very subject.

God says you have to honor your mom and dad's decisions. If they say you can invite only ten girls or you have to invite your cousin Adeline (the one who picks her nose while people are trying to

37

eat), then that's the way it is. Do it graciously (no pouting and slamming of bedroom doors), and the rules might change next time.

God says whenever two or three are gathered together, that's a good thing. If one or two girls have to be left off the list, maybe your mom will let you have them over for a simple sleepover some night soon or perhaps a backyard tea party you can set up yourself.

God says you need to treat other people the way you'd like them to treat you. How would you feel being on the other side of this inviting thing? Would you *want* to be at a party where there were a whole bunch of girls you didn't get along with? Would that make you miserable, or would you welcome the chance to get to know them better? How are you going to treat your guests if you're busy refereeing? Would it be wiser to invite only one group if it means you'll be a better hostess? Stand in your guests' shoes before you make your list.

God says if you have a problem with someone, go and work it out with that person. If you have one friend you'd really like to invite but you're worried that she'll spoil things, have a talk with her. Tell her what you're worried about and describe how you'd like her to behave at your party. Chances are, she doesn't even know she's making things hard for you. Of course, she might also tell you she wouldn't come to your stupid old party now if it were the last one on earth, but you've definitely found out something about her now, haven't you? Have a good cry and get on with the party plans.

CHECK Yourself OUT

Ready to come up with an invitation list? Here's one way to do it.

In the space below, or on another piece of paper, list all the friends you would like to have at a party. Then answer the questions.

1. Write the number you're allowed to invite to your party right next to the star (*). _____ *
2. Think about what kind of party you're having and cross out the names of any friends you're sure wouldn't enjoy themselves. Maybe nonathletic Josie would hate Backyard Olympics. Maybe super-active Molly would climb out of her skin at a field trip to a museum.

Is there anyone on the list you're inviting only because it's the popular thing to do? Do you really like Hayley and feel special about her? Or do you just want to be thought of as being part of her group? If so, cross out those names.

Have you put someone's name down only because if you don't invite her, so-and-so won't come? Cross out that name too. So-and-so can invite that person to *her* party.

What about somebody who is on your list only because if you don't invite her and she finds out about it, she or her mother will have a fit? That name gets crossed off too. Perhaps this confused young'un needs to learn that people who whine and stomp their feet don't get invited to many parties.

Count the names that are left. Have you gotten your list down to the same number you wrote next to the star—or maybe even fewer? If not, go over your list with your mom and ask her opinion. Then pray about it. Sleep on it. (You don't have to literally put it under your pillow!) Pretty soon you'll have a list you're happy with—a list God will be proud of.

Girlz WANT TO KNOW

✿ *LILY: I have a lot of different friends that I know for different reasons, like church, school, my modeling class. I can have only eight girls at my party though, and I'm having trouble deciding. What if I invite this girl from school and that girl from church and another girl from my modeling class—and they all have a terrible time because hardly anybody knows anybody else—and the girls I don't invite get mad at me? Yikes!*

Try limiting your party to just one group, Lily. That way, if you're having a Goofy Make-Over Party for the girls in your modeling class, the girls in your Sunday school class or the ones you hang out with at school will have no reason to be hurt, and everybody at the party will be comfortable and have a blast.

✿ *SUZY: My sister is just a year older than I am. Do I have to invite her to my party? I'm afraid she'll pick at me and then I'll get upset and the whole thing will be ruined.*

The whole family thing can be tough, Suzy. It's always best to be honest and straightforward, so here's the approach I suggest. First, find out if your sister even wants to come to your party. If she's in seventh grade and you're in sixth, for instance, chances are she wouldn't be caught dead hanging out with your not-in-middle-school-yet friends. I wouldn't suggest doing this with a younger sister because they always seem to want to be around the "big girls." If you get the sense that she wants to be there, talk to your mom about your concerns. She might persuade your sister not to horn in on your plans if you present it to Mom calmly and with good reasons. It isn't that you hate your sister's guts—it's just that this party is going to be your day and you'd like to enjoy it without worrying about Sis' behavior. If your mother insists that your sister be included, do two things. One, ask your sister to do a job at the party, like take pictures, serve food, assist you in setting up the games, or be the disc jockey. Two, talk to her about any concerns you have. That doesn't mean—"If you mess up this party for me, so help me I'll snatch you baldheaded!" It means—"Sometimes when I have friends over, you start picking at me and I get really mad. Could you please not do that at this party?" A thank you after the party if she honors your request is definitely in order.

✿ *ZOOEY: I've got my guest list down to size, and I'm leaving out a bunch of girls in my class for really good reasons. But won't they get their feelings hurt or be mad when they see me handing out invitations at school and don't get one?*

They absolutely would, Zooey, which is why it's better to send the invitations through the mail. Handing them out at school, unless everyone in your class is getting one (yikes!), is a surefire way to cause bad feelings.

❀ *RENI: I sent out my party invitations and the day after everybody got theirs, this one girl came up to me at school and got right in my face because I didn't send her one. I didn't know what to say!*

Oh, Reni, that's so hard. It definitely teaches you though, doesn't it, not to do that to the people you know when they give parties? That girl needs to read this book! Since not everybody has good manners when it comes to social things like this, your job is to be gracious. If that happens again, let the person know you understand how she feels and explain to her that you could invite only so many people. If you can say it honestly, tell her she's definitely going to get an invitation next time. If you can't, let it go at that. Disappointment is tough, and it's sometimes even tougher to be the one doing the disappointing, but it's a life thing we all have to experience from time to time. If you handle her nicely, with understanding, this disappointment won't stick with her for long. If she's still mad, tells the whole class you're a selfish brat, and threatens to toilet paper your lawn during the party, you'll know you made a good choice not including her on the list!

I Have My List–NOW WHAT?

This is the fun part! You have some choices to make, but they're all delightful. Just remember as you make them that the invitation you send gives the first impression of your party, so it's the first step toward making it a success. If you take time with the way you invite your guests, they're going to feel special too.

Will you make your invitations or buy them? It's less expensive and definitely more fun to make your own, but there are also some neat ones you can purchase if money isn't a problem and time is. If you decide to make them, the possibilities are endless and the materials are probably right there in your house or can be bought for next to nothing. Here are some ideas.

1. Match your invitation to your theme. If it's a slumber party, make flat "sleeping bags" and slide a paper doll into each one with the party info on her back. If it's a Valentine's Day party, make hearts. If it's a

Mexican fiesta, draw and cut out sombreros. If it's a birthday party, photocopy a baby picture of yourself on paper for making your invitations. These days, lots of people have computer programs with clip art you can use to custom design your invitations.

2. Your invitations don't have to be just paper, you know. If it's a clown party, put the information on a blown-up balloon, deflate it, and send it with a note saying, "Blow Me Up." If it's a swimming party, make tiny towels out of one big one and write your invitation on those. Get the idea?

What are you going to put on your invitations? There are certain things that absolutely have to be included—or your guests will be confused!

- who's giving the party
- the reason for the party
- what kind of party it is
- where it's being held—and include directions if necessary
- when it's being held—date and time it begins *and* ends
- your phone number with a request to let you know if they're coming (more on that below)
- any special information—do they need to dress a certain way, bring anything, prepare something ahead of time, know there's going to be an unusual activity like horseback riding or face painting?

It's fun to write your invitations using words that tie in with your theme. Here's an example:

I'm Launching an Outer Space Party for My Birthday and I want you on Board!

Lift-Off: 2:00 P.M. Saturday, April 9th

Splash Down: 4:00 P.M.

Launching Site: Ashley Parks House
511 Ronald Drive, Smithfield

Come Prepared for the ride of your life! Wear Comfy clothes

A Snack will be served on board.

How will you know how many people are coming? At the bottom of each invitation write RSVP. That stands for *Respondez, s'il vous plait,* which is French for "Answer, if you please." Put your phone number next to that. Keep a guest list near the phone so when people tell you they're coming, you can check their names off. If you're just a few days from party time and haven't received someone's RSVP, call and ask her. You really do need to know how many people are coming. A word of advice: If someone says she can't make it, don't invite somebody else to take her place unless you are absolutely sure she'll never know she wasn't on the original list, and definitely don't ever tell her. It's worse to feel like you're second place than not to be invited at all!

When do I send these babies out? Put your invitations in the mail no more than three weeks and no fewer than ten days before your party. It's good to give people enough time so they don't already have plans but not so much time that they forget.

What if nobody *calls to tell me she's coming?* Every hostess worries about that, but relax. It isn't going to happen. Your invitation is going to be so— well, inviting!—everybody who can will be dying to be there. Give it some time, because some girls may not know about that RSVP thing yet. If you're a week out and nobody's answered, it's fine to simply say, "Did you get my party invitation?"

Talking to God About It

Dear _____, *(your favorite way of address-ing God)*

The idea of inviting people to my very own party is
_____ *(scary, exciting, weird, confusing, etc.) to me. Could you help me out with that feeling?*

I know I can have only so many people, so would you help me put together the best guest list I can? Please make my choices pure, espe-cially about _____ *because she* _____.

And, God, about the invitation thing: my problem with that is (any of these?)

_____ *I'm not sure I can be creative*

_____ *I'm afraid my invitations are going to be lame*

_____ *I might hurt somebody's feelings*

_____ *Maybe nobody will want to come*

_____ *My guests won't get along*

_____ *Somebody will get mad at me*

_____ _____

So, God, please soothe my fears and help me to see things clearly. I know if I just do it all your way, it's going to be wonderful. Help me to listen to what that is.

I love you,

_____ *(your name)*

P.S. You, of course, are invited to my party!

Lily Pad

If I could invite anybody I wanted to my party—alive or dead, famous or not—my guest list would include:

Special Party Feature: THE ULTIMATE THEME PARTY

It Looks Like This: This is a party where everything from the invitations to the games has to do with one theme. Maybe it's a holiday, like Christmas or Valentine's Day. Perhaps it's something you and all of your friends are into, like old Shirley Temple movies or Anne of Green Gables. Historical periods make great themes, everything from medieval times to the 1950s. So do places—like Italy, Mexico, or Hawaii. The reason for the party can be its theme. A going-away party for your friend who's going to Canada for the summer could have a whole travel theme with invitations that look like airplane tickets and disposable cameras for favors. A bash to celebrate your softball team's county championship could be all about ball caps and miniature bats and the whole ballpark fare of peanuts and hot dogs and snow cones. Having a theme makes everything easy to think of, from the invitations to what to wear. It's a blast!

It Takes This Much Space: That depends on the type of party you're throwing and how many people you're having over. A theme party can be held in your breakfast nook or on ten acres! That's the beauty of it.

Guest List: Most people really like the possibilities of a theme party. The only people to steer clear of inviting are those who tend to make fun of clever ideas. They're the ones who roll their eyes in class when you dress up in a toga to give your report on ancient Rome.

Inviting Ideas: It's fun to match your invitation design to your theme, and the possibilities are endless. Just be sure you do it, because your invitation will set the stage for your whole theme and get people into the spirit of it. If you want people to come dressed in poodle skirts and bobby sox for your fifties party, for instance, you'll need to stress the importance of that by making invitations in the shape of old records or pasting the front of a poodle skirt, actually made from felt, on the front of an index card with the party info on it. Prepare your guests for the fun that lies ahead!

Food for Thought: You can really be creative when you're matching party goodies to your theme. Don't you have to have a shamrock-shaped cake and lemon-lime slushes at your St. Patrick's Day doings? Doesn't a night when you're all going to watch *Little Women* mean you need stuff Marmie would have cooked up in her kitchen? And how can you have a French party unless you serve croissants and chocolate mousse? See how a theme cuts down on the decisions you have to make?

Stuff to Do: This is the best part, because just about any game can be adapted to your theme. For a Vacation Party at the end of the school year, pin the tail on the donkey becomes pin the state on the map. For a Goofy Glamour Party, it's nothing but pin the diamond on the tiara. And for a Prairie Party, what else but pin the square on the quilt? The oldest of games gets a fresh twist when you have a theme to wrap it around.

Dressing It Up: By now you've figured out that everything's easier to come up with when you have a theme—and decorations are no exception. Pull out everything you can find around the house that matches your theme and go to town with it. For a Playing in the Snow Party, the eating utensils can be stuffed into mittens at each place at the table.

A snowman made from Styrofoam balls can act as a centerpiece. Wool scarves draped overhead instead of crepe-paper streamers are perfect. Any theme from Colonial America to Underwater World will practically design its own decorations, and your guests will be delighted.

Caution: It's easy to get carried away with a theme party, so keep your antennae up for these warning signs:

- A theme your guests know nothing about. You may be totally into Shakespeare, but inviting your friends to come as their favorite character from one of Shakespeare's plays might draw nothing but blank stares.

- Overkill. A Rain Forest theme is one thing, but don't drown your guests with tree frogs hanging from their drinking straws, tiny plastic monkeys inside every ice cube, and umbrellas they have to carry with them throughout the party. There's a fine line between clever and cheesy. Don't let the theme interfere with the good time you want everyone to have.

- Stressing out when every little thing doesn't tie in with your theme. It's perfectly okay to use plain white napkins at your Memorial Day party if you can't find red, white, and blue ones. So what if your mom won't let you buy little pink slippers as favors for everyone at your Ballet Birthday Party? If you have one item in each category—invitations, decorations, food, and activities—that fits in, you've got yourself a theme party. Remember that the *big* theme is fun. If your friends are having that, your party's a success.

Where's the Food?

**"Bring the fattened calf and kill it.
Let's have a feast and celebrate."**
Luke 15:23

HOW IS THIS A God Thing?

You've known since you were way little that a party isn't a party without food. One of the first things you thought about when the subject of your fifth birthday party came up was probably what kind of cake and ice cream you wanted. Even though a lot of melted rocky road and uneaten mermaid-shaped cake got left on those Little Mermaid paper plates, you'd have cried if your mom had suggested you have a party without those goodies!

Why is food such a big deal in celebrations? God seems to have pretty much made it that way. Let's look at some examples of Bible bashes and see how the eats figured in.

- When God told Samuel he wanted Saul to be the leader of his people, Samuel made sure the feast he prepared for Saul was first-rate. We're talking a big old leg of something. Lamb, maybe? Yum . . . (1 Samuel 9:23–24).
- When the three visitors came to Abraham to tell him that Sarah would have a baby after all, Abraham and Sarah served bread, a calf (which would be veal), curds (*that* sounds pretty disgusting!), and milk (Genesis 18:6–8).
- King Solomon was *always* ready for a party. Every day he was provided with 185 bushels of fine flour and 375 bushels of meal, 10 head of stall-fed cattle, 20 of pasture-fed cattle, 100 sheep and goats, as well as deer, gazelles, roebucks, and choice fowl. Talk about your grocery bills (1 Kings 4:22–23)!

Jesus himself served food at his Last Supper, and he used the bread and the wine as symbols of the sacrifice he was about to make. We're supposed to celebrate often with those same things to remember him and what he did for us.

Look at it this way: Eating good food is one of the best activities God has given us. He knows how much we love good tastes, so what better way to get us smiling and in the celebrating mood than to provide the yummiest food we can think of? At a party, the food rules! (Okay, so maybe it plays a major role.)

So I make a list of my and my friends' favorite foods and that's my menu, right?

Um, not exactly. That menu would look something like this:

- cheese pizza with pepperoni—oh, and pineapple because my friend Kathryn likes that—sausage for Pammie—gotta have mushrooms for Jennifer
- hot dogs, because Susan and Stephanie hate pizza
- Coke, Sprite, Pepsi, Mountain Dew, Dr. Pepper, orange soda, grape soda, and frappuccino—that about covers everybody, except me (I like chocolate milk.)
- French fries
- barbecue potato chips, tortilla chips, and Cheetos; oh, and pork rinds for Shayna; bean dip
- peanut M&Ms, Runts, Skittles, Star Bursts, and Gummy Bears
- ice cream
- marshmallows
- caramel apples

Gotcha. And don't forget the Pepto-Bismol! Yikes! I don't know about you, but that menu sounds like a tummyache waiting to happen. Instead of loading up your menu with favorites that might not like each other too much once they mix together in your stomach, try keeping these things in mind.

1. *How many people will be there?* Remember that you'll need to have enough food for everyone to have at least two servings of everything. If you're serving little party sandwiches, figure five for each person. So if you're having eight girls over, that means sixteen servings of each thing on the menu—or forty little sandwiches! Time, money, and energy start figuring in pretty quickly. The rule of thumb might be, the more people you're inviting, the simpler the food should be. That means if you're giving an Italian party for Columbus Day, you could serve a sit-down spaghetti dinner for four guests, or mini-pizzas for ten. Get the idea?

2. *What kind of party is it?* Some parties are all about the food. The main focus of a tea party, for instance, is sitting around the table drinking tea

and eating pretty goodies. A Pilgrim Feast, an Ice-Cream Social, and a Hawaiian Luau would work the same way. But if your party is centered on going to the Wave Pool or designing homemade Christmas cards, the food is in the background, waiting to round things out. You wouldn't want to have a sit-down meal when everybody's up to her elbows in glitter and paste. That would be the time to serve Christmas cookies and hot chocolate, so people can put on the finishing touches while they munch. See how that works?

3. *How much space do you need to serve it?* If you're having a backyard barbecue and you have a good-sized backyard, go ahead and plan on a long table groaning with burgers and chips and potato salad and baked beans and chocolate cake and watermelon. If you live in a small apartment and you're having a Scrapbook-Making Party, you'll need to limit yourself to some tuna or PB&J sandwiches cut in fun shapes— like the ones your guests will be putting in their scrapbooks! Practically the worst thing in life is a bunch of people jabbing each other with elbows while they're trying to get to the food.

4. *How much money are you allowed to spend*? If you've heard your mom moaning in the grocery store lately, you know that food is expensive. Try not to put your mom in a position where she's scraping the pennies out of the couch cushions to feed your friends gourmet candy. Make a decision about where you want most of your party money to go. If you're giving a Paint Your Own T-Shirt Party, you'll want to spend it on cool paints and other art supplies rather than on ten kinds of snacks everybody will probably be too busy to focus on anyway.

5. *Who's going to prepare and serve it?* It's one thing to plan a feast fit for a king—or at least a half dozen princesses—and another to expect your mom to spend three days in the kitchen preparing it. If you want your mom to make her famous chocolate chip brownies, discuss it with her before you make your final decision. If you have homemade cherry pies in mind for your President's Day party and your mom's favorite thing to make for dinner is reservations at the nearest restaurant, don't even ask her! You may be thinking, "I don't have to worry about any of that because I'm going to do all the cooking myself." That isn't a bad

idea as long as you keep it simple. You may be the youngest gourmet cook in the *Guinness Book of World Records,* but you're still going to have a lot of other things to do to get ready for your event. Why not make it easy on yourself, and your mom, by fixing fun-to-make simple snacks like different kinds of popcorn and sodas for your Movie Party, granola

bars and trail mix for your Hiking Party, or load-up-your-own-hot-dogs and some marshmallows for the Backyard Campfire Party.

6. *What's appropriate for your guest list?* Look at the names of the people you're inviting and think of the way they eat. Do they live for the next meal and dive in like there might not be another one? Those guests need hearty sandwiches and milk shakes. Are they the type to pick at their food and ask what every ingredient is? Better stick with plain pizza and name-brand sodas. Are they girls who are super-creative and will try everything? They'd love to top their own anything, from pizza to ice cream to sandwiches to cookies—and they might even be the right group for introducing some off-the-wall toppings in with the standbys—Canadian bacon, pineapple sauce, pastrami, or old-fashioned sugared almonds.

Whatever you choose, try to keep these basic guidelines in mind.

1. Think about keeping it simple so neither you nor your mom has to be in the kitchen, especially during the party. You'll want to enjoy yourself too, right?

2. Make sure it's convenient. You might be dying to have an ice-cream cake at your birthday party to be held in the park, but how are you going to keep it from melting all over the cooler until it's time to eat it?

3. Consider how much of a mess it could make. As you'll find out in chapter 7, you're going to be doing most of the cleaning up after this little shindig. Do you want to try to get a grape-juice stain off the carpet or be vacuuming up peanut shells until you graduate from high school?

4. The things you do to make the party food look special will make your friends *feel* special. Wouldn't it be cooler to put the chips in a basket than to chuck the bag onto the table? Can you arrange the cookies in a neat pattern on the platter? Have some fun with the goodies and use your imagination.

5. Unless you have a really creative crowd that you've warned beforehand, your party probably isn't the time to serve food your guests aren't familiar with—like artichokes or anchovies or snails. You might think those things are completely cool and delicious, but do you really want to hear comments like, "What is *that* stuff?"

6. Unless your party involves a sit-down meal, serve food that can be eaten standing up. That means nothing that requires a knife and fork or takes two hands to eat.

7. It's better to have too much food than too little.

8. If you're doing the fixing, choose things you can make ahead of time so you can hang out with your guests.

9. Take-out food is okay! Most kids love it anyway, and in today's hectic world, sometimes take-out food is more than okay with your busy mom. Store-bought submarine sandwiches can be fun if you pack them as box lunches with bags of chips and cookies and juice boxes. Take-out fried chicken in a picnic basket, eaten on a blanket on the living room floor, can be a blast. And don't forget the never-ending joys of good old pizza.

One thing we haven't mentioned yet is your food style. After you've thought about all of the above, take a few minutes to consider what kind of food spread will match you, the hostess. This activity will help.

Choose the food in each group that most appeals to you.

For breakfast:

a. heart-shaped waffles topped with flowers made of whipped cream
b. a big stack of pancakes
c. colored cereal made in shapes with marshmallows and other stuff thrown in
d. a piece of toast

For a mid-morning snack:

a. fruit cut up in a crystal goblet
b. a bagel with peanut butter on it
c. crackers I can squirt cheese onto from a can
d. a box of raisins

For lunch:

a. a sandwich cut in the shape of a Hawaiian island with a tiny plastic palm tree stuck in it
b. a bowl of soup, a sandwich, and a bag of chips
c. a Bash Burger—whatever that is, but hey, it sounds fun!
d. a peanut-butter-and-jelly sandwich and a glass of milk

For mid-afternoon snack:

a. tiny oatmeal cookies arranged on a pretty china plate
b. a pile of big oatmeal cookies, maybe with raisins

c. green oatmeal cookies with cool faces on them made from nuts and raisins

d. a couple of oatmeal cookies with no other stuff in them

For supper:

a. chicken breast served in the dining room on the good dishes by candlelight

b. spaghetti served at the kitchen table with a red checkered tablecloth

c. lobster—because I love cracking into it or I want to learn how

d. macaroni and cheese, the kind that comes in a box

For dessert:

a. colorful sherbet served with a silver spoon

b. a big piece of cake and plenty of milk to drink

c. a sundae I could build myself

d. a bowl of ice cream—chocolate, vanilla, or strawberry

Bedtime snack:

a. some grapes; it would be neat if the leaf were still on the little vine, wouldn't it?

b. a big piece of bread with anything I wanted on it

c. a fruit-juice Popsicle I concocted myself earlier in an ice tray

d. a piece of cheese—the kind that comes in slices that are individually wrapped

Okay—count up your a's, b's, c's, and d's. You can put your numbers in these spaces:

_____a   _____b   _____c   _____d

If your highest number was a, you seem to like things fancy. The plate it comes on is almost as important as the food itself! You're really going to enjoy doing beautiful things with the goodies on your table, so go for it. As long as most of your guests share your love for pretty things, don't be afraid to go lacy or flowery or ruffly. Your fanciful table will be a sparkling reflection of you.

If your highest number was b, you probably have a pretty healthy appetite, and you may be envisioning your party with food piled high on trays and in bowls. Go with that! As long as your guests aren't a flock of girls who eat like little birds, they'll enjoy it right along with you. Although you won't be as concerned about how it's presented as the fancy party hostess, don't forget to put those hamburger buns in a fun basket or serve the pizza slices on plates instead of paper towels! Your all-you-can-eat party will shine with the same kind of energy you have.

If your highest number was c, it sounds like you're the creative type. A party gives you a chance to present your food in zany ways, give your friends a chance to build their own, or introduce some out-there treats. Just be careful not to get so carried away with the wildness of it all that you forget it has to taste good too. Save the *really* way-out ideas for the craft projects! If you provide fun food that tastes as good as it looks, your party will be as never-a-dull-moment as you are.

If your highest number was d, food isn't high on your list of the most important things in life. That means it shouldn't be the most important thing at your party either. It's okay to keep it simple. Streamlined is your food style—what a great way to be!

What If Nobody Eats It?

As natural as it is to eat, problems *can* come up with party food. What are the possible pitfalls and what can you do about them?

Girlz WANT TO KNOW

❀ *LILY: All my friends eat differently from each other. How do I find something everybody's going to like?*

If you're having a meal, like lunch or supper, you could serve one plain main dish like hamburgers. Then cover the table with small portions of several different things—a little macaroni salad for Reni and Zooey, a selection of pickles for Kresha, Jell-O for Suzy. You might be surprised at what they'll try from each other's choices once they see them. Remember too that if somebody is so picky that she won't eat anything, it probably wouldn't have mattered what you'd served.

❀ *RENI: Is it okay to ask people to bring food to a party? My mom says it's rude. I think it would be a whole lot easier, and then everybody would be sure to have at least one thing they liked!*

It depends on the kind of party you're having. If everybody in your group says, "I wish we could have a party," and you've volunteered your house, then yes, it's okay to ask each guest to bring something. If you're going to do that, it's a good idea to be specific about what you want, or you could end up with six bags of Doritos and six cans of bean dip. But if your party is all your idea, it is better manners to provide the food yourself. Of course, there are little exceptions—like asking everyone to bring one bag of her favorite snack food to share at a sleepover.

❀ *ZOOEY: On my last birthday, my mom went to all this trouble making lasagna and garlic bread and a salad with all this stuff in it, and people hardly even touched it. Some of them were even whispering and giggling about it at the table. My mom said she was never letting me have another party if my friends were going to behave like that.*

Oops. Some of your guests need to read this book! No matter what is served at a party, nobody should be rude about it, and those whispering gigglers were. Now the girls who didn't eat but didn't criticize the food didn't do anything wrong. It definitely would have been nice if they'd given it a little more of a try, but every family's eating style is different. They may come from homes where the most daring they ever get with food is to order two toppings for their pizza, so a table full of mysterious food wasn't the exciting adventure it was for you. Next time, don't invite the whispering gigglers and plan a little simpler menu. Maybe you'll go with party snacks instead of a big meal, for instance, or serve something you know everybody likes because you've seen them eat it!

Talking to God About It

Before you plan your feast, chat with God about any concerns you have. After all, God's the one who made eating such a big thing in our lives.

Dear _____, *(your favorite way of addressing God)*

I'm thinking about a party, as you know, and I want to make sure I handle it the way you want me to, especially the stuff about the food.

Right now when it comes to what to feed my guests, I'm a little worried about

_____

_____

_____

_____

_____

_____

Would you please help me to know exactly what to do and who to ask for help? Would you help me to keep my head about it and not make it more important than it is? Help me also, would you God, not to try to outdo other people's parties with my feast? Please help me to create a party just to make my friends happy and give them a chance to have fun together and for no other reason.

And while we're talking, God, here's something else I need help with:

_____

_____

_____

_____

_____

_____

Thank you for always being there and being who you are. I know you'll be at my party, right at the table with the rest of us!

Amen,

_____ *(your name)*

Lily Pad

If I could have any kind of food I wanted for my party, I would dream up . . .

Special Party Feature: THE ULTIMATE BIRTHDAY BASH

It Looks Like This: What better reason is there for a party than to celebrate your life on your birthday? At this point in your life, it's about more than eating cake and ice cream and opening presents. It's a time to pick out a theme that matches your personality—be it Career Woman of the Future or Soccer Queen or whatever. It's an opportunity for you to select the food, decorations, and activities you love best and share them with the people you love most. It's a chance to look ahead with excitement to this new year in your life in a way you'll never forget.

It Takes This Much Space: Again, it depends on the number of people you're having and what you plan to do. A birthday party can be an intimate luncheon for four, which can be the ideal time to use an unusual theme you know your three guests will dig—like the Legends of King Arthur or the Chronicles of Narnia or Scrapbook Mania. Or your birthday bash can include all ten people in your Sunday school class for a picnic at the local park and a rousing afternoon of relay games. Choose what fits your personality and your parents' budget.

Guest List: Since most people will bring you a present, unless you ask them not to on your invitation, it's polite to invite only those people you have a relationship with. That girl you have never even spoken to who sits behind you in the computer lab is sure to think you're a little greedy if you ask her to your birthday party unless, of course, you see this as a chance to get to know her. Family members usually like to be included in birthday celebrations, so you'll need to discuss with your mom whether it would be better to have Grandma at your party with your girlfriends or celebrate with the rest of the family that night at dinner. It depends on Grandma's personality and whether she'd enjoy an afternoon of listening to you and your friends giggle!

Inviting Ideas: It's important on birthday invitations to say that the party's for your birthday. It's embarrassing for a guest to show up without a gift when everyone else has brought you one. Of course, if you don't want your friends to shower you with presents, be plain about that on the invitation—and if someone brings one anyway, thank her privately and set it aside to open with just her later.

Food for Thought: Cake and ice cream are the traditional birthday party fare, but if you'd prefer something else, go for it! Candles can be stuck into anything from giant cookies to ice cream sundaes. It doesn't even have to be a dessert. Can you envision a birthday pizza? A platter of burgers? A dish of lasagna? If you have a theme, pick out yummy food that matches it and plug in candles or sparklers or a photocopy of that picture of you covered in frosting on your first birthday! Then eat up and enjoy. If you do have cake, have matches on hand for lighting candles, and make sure you have a big enough cake for everyone to have a generous slice. If you serve an ice-cream cake, take it out of the freezer and put it in the refrigerator forty-five minutes before you're going to eat it so it won't be so hard to cut.

Stuff to Do: Be sure you have activities planned just as for any other party. Opening presents and eating will take less than an hour, and you'll want to save those for the end of the party anyway. Find games or activities that fit your theme (which we'll talk about in chapter 5). If you really want the focus to be on the celebration of life, you can ask everyone to give you a baby picture of herself several days before the party and make a display of them with each one numbered. The person who matches the most baby pictures correctly to their more grown-up faces wins. You can also play What's My Future, where you decorate and label five bags—Name, Career, Where You Live, Who Lives with You, and Favorite Hobby. Have each girl write her name on a piece of paper and put it in the Name bag. Then have each person write something bizarre for each bag. "Predict" each girl's future as she pulls one slip of paper out of each bag. Then liven things up with dress-up clothes from the attic or the Salvation Army and have a We Are the Future parade with a prize for each guest—Most Creative, Most Hilarious, Most Off-the-Wall, and so forth. Or you can celebrate life by sharing your favorite activity with your friends, be it miniature golf or giving each other manicures, as long as it's something your guests will be able to enjoy right along with you.

Dressing It Up: A birthday party is one of the times when it's especially appropriate to go all out with decorations if that's your thing. After all, this is your life you're celebrating! If you have a theme, chapter 6 will help you. If not, try decorating in your favorite colors. Or put a collection of pictures from each year of your life on the table. Or make a display representing all your interests—maybe your snorkeling mask, your tap shoes, and your collection of stuffed frogs. This is a good time to show who you're becoming!

Caution:

- Remember that your guests' needs and desires come first even though it's your birthday.
- When you're opening presents, be sure the giver is there before you open her gift. Open the card first and read it, silently if you want to. Don't toss the card aside and tear into the present like a dog digging up a bone! Make a positive comment about the gift, even if you hate it, already have one, or can't tell what it is. Never say, "Oh, I already have one of these," or "What am I supposed to do with this?" or "Since when was I into Barbies?" Show respect for the gift and the guest. You can try things like "I've never seen anything like this! How cool!" or "I never expected one of these. Thanks, Jenna," or "This is an interesting color. I don't have anything like this—I can't wait to try it on."
- If before the party someone asks what you'd like to have for a present, give suggestions. People wouldn't ask if they didn't want to know. But

keep your suggestions inexpensive. "Anything from the Gap," isn't the best answer. Think of things that cost around five dollars, and certainly no more than ten dollars. "I love markers," you might say, "and I use them up so fast." Or, "I'm into cool socks or things to put in my hair. You can't miss with stickers—I still put them on everything!"

- Do not under any circumstances talk about the price of a gift you receive. And, of course, don't make more of a fuss over a gift that is obviously expensive than you do over something somebody lovingly picked out for you at the dollar store.
- Don't forget those thank-you notes (see chapter 7) even though you've thanked each person after you've opened her gift.
- If somebody shows up without a gift, don't point that out. Act as if you didn't notice. If somebody else blurts out, "Hey, what did Heidi give you?" answer with, "She's here, and that's all I care about," and then quickly change the subject.
- If the whole singing "Happy Birthday" thing embarrasses you, talk to your mom about it beforehand and come up with something else to make your birthday official. Maybe you can write a simple prayer to say when the cake comes out, or simply blow out the candles and then as the cake's being cut, tell each guest why you're glad she's in your life. If someone says, "How come we didn't sing 'Happy Birthday'?" smile and say, "I wanted to do something different." After all, it is *your* birthday!

Games That Aren't Lame

When the men were returning home after David
had killed the Philistine, the women came out from
all the towns of Israel to meet King Saul with
singing and dancing, with joyful songs and with
tambourines and lutes.

1 Samuel 18:6

What are we gonna do at your party?"

That's a question you're bound to hear as soon as your invitations go out. Of course! Nobody wants to just sit around nibbling cookies.

So be ready with an answer that'll have everybody counting the days until party time. First, let's see what God has to say about it.

GAMES ARE A God Thing?

Having a good time is definitely a God thing. God's people all over the Bible—our role models—showed their joy by playing. We're talking singing, dancing, and making music on everything from harps, lyres, and tambourines to cymbals, trumpets, and coolest of all, ram's horns. Quite a bit of shouting was going on—not to mention palm waving. They were into games too, especially foot races with big prizes.

"Go and enjoy choice food and sweet drinks, and send some to those who have nothing prepared," the prophet said in Nehemiah 8:10. "This day is sacred to our Lord. Do not grieve, for the joy of the LORD is your strength." You probably won't be *aware* that you're celebrating God when you're playing charades or smacking at a piñata with your guests. But the laughing and squealing and hooting shows you're enjoying the life God has given you. As the hostess who comes up with fun stuff to do, you're treating God's other kids to some joy. God appreciates that.

So What Makes Good Party Play?

Glad you asked. No matter what activities you plan for your get-together—whether it's taking a hike up a hill for a picnic or playing round-robin board games in your family room—there are certain qualities all great party doings share. Here they are.

• They're planned ahead. All the stuff needed is right there. The hostess isn't standing around trying to think of something to do while everyone yawns or throws popcorn.

- An ice-breaker activity opens the event to get people relaxed and into a party frame of mind as soon as they arrive, especially if some people don't know each other already. If you're having an International Party, for instance, maybe you'll have a table set up with art stuff so each guest can make her own "passport" as she arrives. As everyone gathers at your house for a birthday trip to the circus, each new arrival can add to decorating the giant clown you have on a big piece of white paper up on the wall. It keeps your guests from standing around feeling awkward, waiting for the party to begin.

- Plans include some active games (like musical chairs, where you can't just walk around; you have to imitate an animal motion); some quiet activities (like making cool hats); some physical games (like balloon tag, where everyone ties a balloon to her ankle, and you all try to pop each other's without using your hands), and some mental games (like coffeepot, where the group chooses an action word and the person who's "It" has to guess what the word is by asking such questions as "Do I coffeepot in school?"). Alternate the type of activities, and the party will never drag.

- Activities are demonstrated before they're started.

- The games fit the party theme. Having an Egyptian Party? Play wrap the mummy! (You have two-person teams. One person is the mummy, and the other is the wrapper. The first pair to complete the wrapping of the mummy with unbroken toilet paper so no skin is showing wins!) Having a Goofy Glamour Night? Put various "glamour items" (like really wild lipstick, bizarre hats, or glitzy jewelry) in paper bags. Divide into teams and have each team give one girl on the team a "makeover," using only the items in the bag.

- Competitiveness does not take over. The guests are there to have fun, not to knock themselves out! A light game of volleyball played with a beach ball works better than a serious soccer match, even if all your guests are soccer champs. A party is a time to lighten up a little.

CHECK Yourself OUT

Which of these three parties do you think was probably the most successful?

Lily's Luau

At Lily's Hawaiian Party, she met each guest at the door with a lei (you know, one of those flower necklaces) to put around their necks. Each girl was allowed to design her own hula skirt (from green crepe paper and an assortment of fake flowers) and an anklet (from beads and thin leather cord). Then they had a goofy hula move contest that was hilarious, especially since her dad videotaped it and they watched it later. That was followed by a game of limbo and "surfing" down the hill in her backyard with garbage-bag "surfboards." While they were settling down, waiting for the food to be served, they played a game called guess what this hawaiian word means. Some of their definitions were a riot!

Reni's Rodeo

At Reni's Country-Western Party, she asked everybody to dress up country-western style, and she gave each girl either a red or a blue bandana to wear when she arrived. First, she had her cousin from Nashville teach everybody how to line dance. Then they had a horse race in the backyard (the "horses" were tricycles). Then they divided into teams (red bandanas and blue bandanas), and one team had to try to "rope" all the players on the other team in a certain period of time. Next came the tug of war, and finally, the barrel-racing relay, which they had to do on foot blindfolded! They all ate out of cute little mess kits, sitting astride sawhorses with blanket "saddles" on them.

Suzy's Sewing Party

At Suzy's Sewing Party, she had a bunch of scraps of different kinds of material with numbers on them. Each guest was given a piece of paper and a pencil and asked to name as many types of fabric as she could; the winner got a little purse sewing kit. Then they played scissors crossed, which is played sitting in a circle, trying to figure out a scissors-passing code. Finally, she had a table set up with all kinds of sewing supplies, and she let each girl take what she wanted to make a little project that she demonstrated. Girls who didn't want to sew could look through her pile of fashion magazines.

Which one did you pick? _____

Of course, there is no right or wrong answer, but here are some things to be aware of.

Suzy's Sewing Party was unusual and definitely centered around a theme. But if everyone she invited wasn't into sewing, it was a disaster waiting for a moment to happen! Not only that, but all of her planned activities were low-key, quiet, sit-down kinds of things. Again, that could work for the right kind of group. Let's hope Suzy was careful with her guest list!

Reni's Rodeo was wild and definitely had a lot of action! If all her guests were nonstop bundles of energy, it could have worked, but even the liveliest partygoers need a breather in there. Dude, they were slamming from one activity to another, and each one was more physical and active than the one before it. They even had to sit on "horses" to eat! All her games, except the line dancing, were competitive too. Whew! I bet they were ready for the bunkhouse when they left that party!

Lily's Luau was probably the most successful. She alternated quiet games and active ones—some that called for physical activity and some that asked her guests to be creative. Only the goofy hula move contest was competitive, but that was too much of a hoot for anybody to get too serious about winning. She let them wind down right before they ate so they could enjoy their food and enjoy watching the video and replaying every minute.

And the Winner Is . . . !

If you *are* going to have winners in your games, ya gotta have prizes. Here are some things to remember about the trophy thing.

- Give out prizes for a lot of different activities, and even give different categories of prizes—like one for the best sport, for instance. That gives everybody a chance to be a winner.
- Plan some games and activities that require no prizes so everybody's focus isn't on "what can I win?"
- Keep the prizes inexpensive—things like all-day suckers at your Old-Fashioned Ice-Cream Social, big peppermint sticks at your Christmas party, and fun toothbrushes at your sleepover. If the prizes didn't cost $10.95 at Toys-R-Us, the people who lose at games won't feel bad.
- You can also give fun medals or badges you've made yourself or bought at a party store.

Here's another idea for you: Why not forget prizes and play the games for fun—then give every guest a party favor when she leaves?

The tradition of giving favors to guests started way back in medieval times when a lady or a prince would give a "favor" to a certain friend or knight. They were usually ribbons or gloves or a small piece of jewelry. That's where the word *favorite* comes from: Those who received such favors were called favorites. Cool, huh?

The custom lives on when a hostess gives favors to her guests to show her appreciation for their coming. They don't have to be big or expensive— just a little something for each guest to take home to remind her what a good time she had at your party. It's really fun to make them—think of what you can do and like to do. Of course your party theme will give you ideas. Here are some to get you started.

- At a pool party, give cheap, crazy sunglasses as favors.

- At a backyard carnival, give everybody a balloon hat to take home.
- Having a party with an Asian flair? Send everyone off with a little origami figure.
- Did you all go to the zoo for your birthday party? Give each girl a tiny animal figure.
- Was it a sledding party in your backyard? Dip plastic spoons in chocolate and harden them in the fridge. Wrap in colorful plastic wrap and ribbon for guests to stir their hot chocolate with later while they reminisce about the fun they had.

Remember this! It's become a huge deal in some places to send every guest home with a goody bag filled to the brim with favors. Don't feel as if you have to do that. Giving parties isn't a competition! Do what's fun for you and what you think would be fun for your guests, but don't think you absolutely must beg your mom to spend a gazillion dollars on bags of stuff just because other people are doing it. That definitely isn't a God thing.

What If the Games Get Lame?
Girlz WANT TO KNOW

✿ *LILY: What if it's time to switch to another game and nobody wants to because they like the one we're playing?*

Then stick with it! If it works, go ahead and start another round. The trick is to move to the next thing as soon as you see anybody getting tired of what you're doing. Finish that round and start something fresh.

✿ *RENI: What if I start a game and they all hate it?*

Make sure everybody understands how the thing is played, because sometimes when people immediately turn their noses up at something, it means they don't get how it's done. Then go ahead and start the game and give it a few minutes. If it doesn't get off the ground and people start scowling or parking themselves on the sidelines, change to something else. That's why it's good to have more planned than you're going to do, just in case. And remember, if something doesn't work out, it isn't a tragedy. I mean, who knew they wouldn't want to have a mud-pie-eating contest, right? (Some people are so picky!)

✿ *ZOOEY: What if people start fighting, like over who won?*

Don't you hate that? It's way bad manners, but if it happens, there's a way to deal with it. As hostess, don't take sides. Give them each a prize and start a new game right away. This isn't the place to teach people lessons—this is a party. Make sure your non-fighting guests get the good time they deserve.

Just Do It

Now comes the fun part! Think about all we've talked about, and then see if you can come up with your own party game plan, even if you aren't planning a party right now. You've got the Ultimate Game Planning Sheet to help you! If you like how this turns out, transfer your ideas to the Ultimate Party Planning Sheet in the back of the book.

Talking to God About It

Dear _____, *(your favorite way of addressing God)*

It's so fun thinking about party games, Lord, but I want to make sure I do it with good judgment and with care for other people's feelings. Will you help me?

I'm especially concerned about
this kind of game: _____
these certain people: _____
what I'll do if _____
I believe you'll help me, God, with everything I need in order to
show my friends a good time at my party—because I know you love a
good time too!
Amen,
_____ *(your name)*

Lily Pad

The perfect game would be one where . . .

_____
_____
_____
_____
_____
_____
_____
_____
_____
_____
_____

Special Party Feature: THE ULTIMATE COSTUME GIG

It Looks Like This: This is one of the most fun kinds of parties to give because your guests get into the spirit of the thing before the day of the party as they decide what to wear. Of course, for some people that can be an over-whelming choice, so you can help by giving your costume party a more specific theme—"Come as your favorite cartoon character," or "Come dressed as what you want to be in the future," or "Let us guess your famous person's name." When everybody shows up in costume, the party room comes alive with laughing and guessing. It's a blast.

It Takes This Much Space: This is not the time to cram a bunch of people into a small area, because you may be faced with angel wings, Darth Vader capes, and Scarlett O'Hara hoop skirts. Get your mom and dad to help you figure out if you can have at least six square feet for each guest. Consider having your party outside, in the basement, or in the garage if you don't have a big family room or recreation area.

Guest List: Most of the time, costume parties are more fun when there are ten or more people. There are exceptions, of course. If you and three of your friends are into *Little Women* and want to dress as the four sisters and sit down to an intimate tea, you'll have a lovely time. A costume party, if it's not your birthday, is a good time to invite people you don't know well but would like to get to know better. There's something about wearing a costume that helps erase shyness.

Inviting Ideas: Be sure to give your guests at least two weeks' notice about your party. They have some preparing to do! Be clear about your theme. On the invitation, encourage your guests to make their own costumes so nobody thinks she has to go to a rental store for something elaborate. You could even indicate that if anyone has trouble coming up with a costume, you have great ideas. Then get yourself a make-your-own-costume book from the library and read up so you can give suggestions. It will be fun to design your invitation to match your theme. Maybe get a bunch of cheapo masks that go over the eyes and write the party info on those, or make some out of paper. Or do something to represent your specific theme: "Come Dressed for the Islands" might be written on a little cardboard surfboard. "You're Invited to a

Little House on the Prairie Hoedown" might be written on a card that's been covered on the outside in calico fabric. Have a ball with this!

Food for Thought: Costumes can be cumbersome to eat in, so keep the food simple. A sit-down meal isn't the best idea (Renaissance sleeves get dragged through the gravy, masks fall off into the spaghetti sauce—that kind of thing). Better to do stand-up snacks where people can wander with a plate of no-mess refreshments and concentrate on staying in character, which is way fun. You can still match snacks to theme. Goldfish crackers and little tuna sandwiches would work for your Dress for the Seashore Party (the one you're giving in February to lift everybody out of the winter doldrums). How about fancy pastries for your Come Dressed as Your Favorite Fantasy Party? They don't even have to come from a bakery—most grocery stores have fun stuff made fresh every day for a lower cost.

Stuff to Do: The costumes themselves will be the main focus of your party. You can have a costume parade—complete with videotaping if you want—and let either your family or the guests themselves vote. It would be good to prepare a prize—like a ribbon such as the ones they give at fairs—for each guest, using categories like Most Likely to Get a Laugh or Most Unusual. If you have zany friends, each one can tell about herself in character, or you can ask each girl to be her character while you all have tea or play a game and then see who can guess the most characters correctly. A good prize might be one of those wonderful costume paper-doll books. If you do plan other activities—and you probably should—make sure they can be done comfortably in costume or tell guests ahead of time to bring other clothes to change into.

Dressing It Up: A costume party requires the least decorations of almost any celebration because the costumes themselves dress up the space. It's fun to set the stage with perhaps one big piece. Could you have a starship hanging from the ceiling over the refreshment table for your Come As Your

Favorite Star Trek Character Party? What about a nice big flower arrangement for your Victorian party? Once your guests arrive in their getups, the room will come alive with décor!

Caution:

- Keep the pre-party bustle for costumes fun. Reassure your friends who are stressing about their outfits. Encourage all guests to use their imaginations and make their costumes. Make yours, in fact. Play down competitive talk like, "I want to have the best costume there," or "Everybody's just gonna fall over when they see me." It's a celebration—not a contest.
- Give every guest that same attention for her costume when she comes in. Avoid saying things like, "That's cute, Jenny. You oughta see what Becky has on though."
- Have the photographer take pictures or videos early in the party, before costumes get hot and uncomfortable and guests start peeling them off!
- Suggest that everyone take off masks before eating, drinking, or playing lively games. That'll help avoid spills and accidents.
- Remember that even the smallest negative remark can hurt feelings. Think before you blurt out, "So what are *you* supposed to be?" Your party should be about having fun—not being an exact replica of Nancy Drew (or whoever you're dressed as)!

Decorate!

"You are to take choice fruit from the trees, and
palm fronds, leafy branches and poplars, and
rejoice before the LORD your God.... Celebrate
this as a festival to the LORD."

Leviticus 23:40–41

Do you love to go to the mall at Christmas time when it's all decorated with huge ornaments and garlands of tinsel the size of towrope? Do your eyes sparkle when you see a table set for dinner with candles and flowers and napkins that match the tablecloth? Do you really get into plastering hearts on the front windows for Valentine's Day, turkeys for Thanksgiving, big old lilies for Easter?

If you answered yes to any of those questions, it's probably because decorations help get us into the mood for the upcoming celebration. Christmas would still be Christmas without the wreath on the door, and the Fourth of July would still happen if the American flag weren't flying out in front of your house. But don't those things get you excited about what's ahead? One look at the Stars and Stripes flapping in the breeze off the front porch and you can almost taste the watermelon and hear the fireworks.

That's why decorations *can* be a fun part of any party—because they get the guests psyched up for all the cool stuff the hostess has planned. They can immediately erase all thoughts of not getting to sit in the front seat on the way to the party or having to go home and do math homework when the party's over. They can transport every guest into a party world that leaves the whole, complicated real world outside for a while.

HOW IS THIS A God Thing?

God's been into making a great environment since Creation! Think about the Garden of Eden, where he planted "trees that were pleasing to the eye" (Genesis 2:9) and put in gold and onyx. He even remembered to make it smell good with "aromatic resin" (Genesis 2:12).

Think about God displaying a rainbow in the clouds to reassure Noah—and us (Genesis 9:12–16)!

Think about God describing to Moses the sanctuary he wanted the Israelites to make for him. We're talking an ark overlaid with pure gold and gold molding around it (Exodus 25:11); a tabernacle "with ten curtains of finely twisted linen and blue, purple and scarlet yarn, with cherubim worked into them by a skilled craftsman" (Exodus 26:1); an altar overlaid with bronze (Exodus 27:2), and a court-yard with posts made with silver bands (Exodus 27:17).

Think about the temple he had Solomon build (1 Kings 6), and the one he instructed David to make preparations for (1 Chronicles 22).

Even Jesus' description of heaven gives us a peek at a wonderful place: a mansion with many rooms that are being prepared just for us (John 14:1–4).

Of course, even though the Bible is filled with beautiful places, that isn't *all* it's filled with. It's the same with a party: It isn't *all* about the decorations. But even the smallest bit of attention to the pretty bowl you put the chips in or the balloons you hang from the light fixture over the table says to your guests, "I've prepared a place just for you!" I don't know about you, but as a guest, I really dig that.

How Much of a Big Deal Do I Make Out of Balloons and Streamers?

The answer to that question depends on several things, which we'll get to in a minute. The first one is probably the most important, and that's you and your own party style.

Here's a list of the things that make up the ultimate bash. Number them in order of how important they are to you, with number 1 being the most important and number 6 being the least important. Remember, there are no right or wrong answers. Number them the way you think of them.

_____ what you're going to have to eat

_____ what the invitations look like

_____ what you're going to wear as the hostess

_____ what games or activities you'll have

_____ how the party space will look

_____ what party favors you'll give out

If "how the party space will look" is for you:

Number 1 or 2—You'd really like to go wild with the decorations. You probably have visions of turning the backyard into an exact replica of a desert island for your Shipwrecked Party or at least your family room into a winter wonderland for your Let's Beat the January Blues Bash. Consider lots of stuff before you drag your mom to the Parties-R-Us store, but until we get to those, dream on. Many things are possible!

Number 3 or 4—You probably hadn't thought about it too much before, but now that we mention it, yeah, it might be fun to booby trap the living room for your April Fool's Party or put a poster of France on the front door for your Café Paris lunch. You won't want to put the decorations before whatever you named as number 1 and number 2, but if there's time and some money left over (more on this in a minute), give the look of your party space some thought.

Number 5 or 6—You might be just as happy without any decorations, and that's perfectly okay. But if—now that we've mentioned it—it does sound kind of neat to cover the front door with a beach towel for your swimming party or put a giant pencil on the middle of the table for your Back-to-School gig, go for it. But do the stuff you're really jazzed about first, like the games and the food, and if you don't get around to cool decorations, don't worry about it. They're fun, but for you they aren't everything.

And You Know What Else About Decorations?

Here are the things to think about as you decide whether to go bananas with streamers and twinkly lights or be content with a bowl of peanut M&Ms to liven up the table.

- *Do decorations fit your budget?* Talk to your mom about how much is already being spent on food, favors, invitations, and items for games. If you want to transform your party room into Wonderland for your Mad Hatter Tea Party and Mom says her wallet is empty, see what you can find around the house to use, with her permission of course. What about those funky chairs up in the attic? Can you mix and match teapots and cups and saucers and colored napkins? Can you make a banner that says, "Happy Un-birthday!"? Using your imagination is a lot more fun than buying out the party aisle at Wal-Mart.

- *How much time will there be for putting up decorations or arranging the room the day of the party?* You definitely don't want to still be blowing up balloons when your guests arrive.

- *Who's available to help you?* You might have visions of stringing white lights all over the patio for a Fairy Tale effect, but if your mom's going to be in the kitchen making the angel food cake and your dad is taking your little brothers and sisters to Chuck E. Cheese's to keep them occupied—who does that leave? Be prepared to adapt your original idea and accept "No, my love, you cannot climb up on that ladder by yourself" as the final word.

- *Whom are you inviting?* Are your guests the type who will ooh and ah over your efforts to turn your family room into a Mexican fiesta, or are they likely to pick up the sombreros and use them as Frisbees? If you think decorations will make both you and your friends happy, go for it. If you think it's a waste of time because they'll be much more interested in the fact that your cousin the dancer is going to teach everyone salsa dancing, then settle for one big sombrero on the table with the chips and guacamole and let it go at that.

- *How do decorations fit in with your theme or activities?* If you're planning to play indoor volleyball with Nerf balls in the rec room, you probably won't want to hang streamers that will come down with the first serve. On the other hand, if you've promised an authentic Night with Disney where you're going to watch Disney movies, not to have movie posters and Disney characters hanging around the room would be wasting a perfect opportunity!

Get the Idea?

Just in case you don't, maybe the Girlz can help you get your imagination going.

Girlz WANT TO KNOW

✿ *LILY: I totally want to go all out and decorate the entire house for my birthday party, but my mom thinks having the bakery decorate the cake is going all out. Help!*

That doesn't surprise us, Lily! You do everything 200 percent! And you still can—you just need to shift your vision a little. Remember that too many decorations can look overwhelming and take the focus away from the fun stuff you're going to be doing at your party. All you're trying to do is set a mood. That ought to get you down to a room or two. Now think in terms of one big central focus that will draw attention and convince people they really are where you want them to be. They'll fill in the rest with their imaginations. Let's say your theme is We Are the Stars of the Future. Instead of turning the entire family room into something out of Star Wars, get a huge piece of cardboard (maybe from a box a refrigerator comes in) or a piece of plywood, cover it with aluminum foil or silver cloth, and then make star-shaped frames out of bright sparkly paper and put them on your silver board. On a table near the door where guests will be arriving, have materials for them to draw how they see themselves in the future, and put the drawings in the frames. Voila! An instant—big—decoration they'll come back to again and again during the party. Stars hanging from the ceiling might add that overall look you're going for. Get the idea?

✿ *RENI: My party's going to be in the backyard, and we can't decorate that much out there, but I still want it to look like there's a party going on. I'm jazzed about this whole decoration thing!*

That's easily solved. Your guests will probably have to come through the house, right? Make a party sign for your front door that's totally done up to match your theme. For your backyard shindig, you could make it in the shape of a big beach umbrella, a giant hot dog in a bun, or a huge smiling sun. Print RENI'S BEACH BASH in bold letters. Then if you want to go even further, decorate the entrance area just inside the front door. Put a basket of beach balls and towels there. Put twinkly lights on a big potted plant. Hang bright-colored fish cutouts from the ceiling. Then, to make sure everybody knows she's on the right track for the back door, tape big bare-feet cutouts on the floor leading to the door where the party fun begins. Decorate near that door too. Set up a basket of cheap, bright sunglasses for each guest to select from before emerging into the sun or tack sun hats around the doorway. Be creative with whatever you have around the house. By the time your guests do get to the backyard, they'll have just the image in mind you want them to have.

✿ *ZOOEY: I don't have a problem with decorations—it's the space I gotta worry about. My mom's all freaked out that somebody's going to wander into another part of the house instead of staying in the party area and either get into something or get hurt. I keep telling her we aren't three years old, but she's still freaking out.*

Help her to freak no more by taking these simple precautions. They won't insult anybody, and they'll calm Mom right down.

- Close all the doors to rooms that are off limits. Most people won't wander into rooms that aren't open.
- Make sure all your guests know where the bathroom is that they can use, or tape bright arrows on the floor to show the way.
- Put away breakable items that mean a lot to your mom—like that vase that was her great-great-grandmother's.
- Put away stuff that could be dangerous, like fireplace tools or knives that are usually displayed on the kitchen counter.
- Put away remote-control units.
- Provide paper cups on the bathroom sink and put extra toilet paper on the

floor under the dispenser—then no one has to root around in closets or cabinets.

- Keep your guests so busy and happy and things moving along so smoothly that no one will want to wander around!

✿ *KRESHA: We have no money for decorations—I'm lucky to be having a party at all—and my mom and I aren't creative. If we try to make something, it's going to look stupid. I'm thinking of not having the party at all—but I really want to!*

Never fear—that's what friends are for! Have a "pre-party" party the night before. Invite one or two of your creative friends over for simple snacks and decorating—and perhaps to spend the night if that doesn't sound overwhelming to you and your mom. Tell them about your theme ahead of time so they can be thinking about ideas. Then gather everything you can find in your house that looks like it might go with your theme, get the party room clean, and then go for it. Here are two ideas to get you started.

- For an autumn party where you're going to eat popcorn and bob for apples and roast marshmallows in your fireplace, find as many pretty fall leaves as you can and put them in baskets. Tape leaves around the doorway to the party room and scatter them on the table. Dress all the sofa pillows in sweaters and arrange them around the fireplace for guests to sit on. Put some leaves in a big basket and set it in a corner next to the leaf rake. Make a scarecrow out of leaves stuffed in garbage bags and sit him in a chair. Cool, huh?
- For a Back-to-School Party, cover the front door with a dark green sheet and pin white letters on it to look like a chalkboard. Make an arrangement with books, a lunch box, a backpack, and maybe a pennant in your school's colors for the entrance area. Borrow your little brother's toy school bus for the table centerpiece. Tie a pencil to each set of plastic spoon

and knife. Hang these kinds of things from the ceiling or arrange them in various spots around the room: ruler, Elmer's glue bottle, craft scissors, pocket calculator, dictionary, or an assignment pad. Use a big piece of white paper to cover the table and write multiplication problems on it with markers. Make miniature report cards to use as place cards at the table if you're going to sit down for a meal.

Talking to God About It

Dear _____, (your favorite way of addressing God)
I'm excited about creating a different world for the guests at my party. I guess it's sort of like the way you feel when you make a wonderful place for one of us. But I'm unsure about some things. Will you help me out? The things I've put little crosses next to below are the ones I really pray you'll assist me with—big time!

_____Being realistic with my plans
_____Not whining and begging if my parents say no to something I want to do with my party space
_____Working with what I have
_____Being creative
_____Being willing to ask for help
_____Taking the responsibility to help with the not-so-fun parts like cleaning
_____Taking the responsibility for making sure my guests respect our home
_____Remembering that the rest of the family has to live in our house while I'm transforming it
_____Making sure it's a fun celebration and not a chance for me to show off

I believe in your help, God. I'm already thanking you!

Amen,
_____ (your name)

Lily Pad

If I could transform the whole house for my party, I would . . .

Special Party Feature:
THE ULTIMATE BOY-GIRL GET-TOGETHER

It Looks Like This: This is a party where both boys and girls are invited—obviously! Everything's designed to make both types feel comfortable with these odd creatures of the opposite sex! The only difference between this and an all-girl gig is that you'll have to consider the peculiarities of boys in the planning. Usually, though not always, they tend to be rowdier and need more space, eat more, and are totally impatient with anything that's too "girlie." It doesn't take a brain surgeon to figure out that a boy-girl get-together is not the time to have a tea party, a sleepover (duh!), a sewing circle, or a craft night (unless the crafts are boy-proof and "cool"). If you know and like boys well enough to want them at your party, then you'll know what kind of shindig to throw. But once you've decided, check out the idea with some males you trust. After all, it would be pretty embarrassing to have a bunch of guys sitting around yawning or even worse, making up their own game of push the cupcake into your buddy's face.

It Takes This Much Space: As we just mentioned, boys seem to need more elbow room for all that action that seems to constantly be going on with them. If you have a big backyard, a large recreation or family room, or a garage that's pretty spacious when the cars aren't in there, you're fine. Girls don't seem to mind being cozy. Boys—they're a whole different animal (or haven't you noticed)!

Guest List: It's a good idea to keep your first boy-girl thing fairly small—like ten or under—and to make the numbers even. If you have eight girls and two boys, those two boys are going to clump together like lumps of cream of wheat, and you probably couldn't get them to play a game with those eight girls if you paid them. You'll want to invite boys who are comfortable with girls and vice versa. Even if a boy is the cutest thing who ever walked the face of the earth, if he's also the boy who cuts everybody down every time he opens his mouth, he doesn't belong on your guest list. If a girlfriend of yours is so boy crazy she can barely write her name without +Bryan or +Michael after it, she probably shouldn't make the cut either. What you're looking for is a combination of guys and girls who will get along and discover that those other-gender people can make pretty good friends.

Inviting Ideas: Guys aren't as big on cutesy invitations as girls are. That doesn't mean you should bag your creative ideas because you have boys on your list. Just either (a) make your invitation something that will appeal to both boys and girls (no ruffles, lace, or flowers) or (b) be prepared for some boy to say, "I'm not coming. It sounds like a sissy party." Invitations with bright colors, action, cool shapes, or characters who are currently "in" should catch everybody's eye.

Food for Thought: Watch how boys eat in the lunchroom at your school and plan accordingly! Boys seem to like plainer food—hot dogs, pizza, hamburgers, ice cream, junk snacks—and lots of it. Not that girls aren't, but boys can be even pickier about "what's in it?" If you want to go all out with cake decorations and fancy cookies, go ahead, but don't expect any of your male guests to squeal over them. Boys have been known to like the build-your-own idea. Just be sure you have plenty of everything, because they can sure put away the groceries.

Stuff to Do: You'll want to have a well-prepared agenda of activities and start them as soon as the first guest gets there. (See our discussion of icebreakers in chapter 5.) That will keep the girls from gathering on one side of the room and the boys on the other. It's amazing how boys who run up and down the aisles in the classroom stealing girls' pencils and hiding their backpacks will become so shy at a party it's as if they've had a personality transplant. Ya gotta keep them busy. They won't do well standing around talking and snacking. We've already talked about varying your activities to include some active and some quieter ones, so you know your party doesn't have to be nonstop, full-out action the entire time. Just don't let more than a few minutes pass between games, and make the active ones longer than the quieter ones. Beware of anything too rough; boys are so used to playing among themselves, they don't always realize that females probably have never been thrown to the ground and put in a stranglehold in their lives!

Dressing It Up: Boys can be pretty impressed by the bigger stuff—the huge pile of hay in the corner at your autumn-fest, for instance. They also like unusual things—like an entire refrigerator box of Styrofoam peanuts to jump into. But keep in mind that the balloons, table centerpiece, and mirror ball hanging from the ceiling are for your girlfriends. Go ahead and decorate though. Your party is for the girls too. It isn't just an excuse to invite boys over!

Caution: Having boys at a party can change the way everybody acts, but that doesn't have to be a bad thing. It means you'll want to be aware of these things.

- Sometimes girls get giddy when boys are around—go figure—and the whispering and gossiping start. Try to keep your guests so busy having fun that no one has time for that. If you see your girlfriends in the corner pointing at the boys and giggling, herd them back to the group with an activity they can't resist.
- Believe it or not, girls are as much a mystery to boys as boys are to girls, and that can make them pretty uncomfortable. So when a bevy of girls all go to the restroom at the same time, boys can't help but squirm, wondering what they're talking about in there. Discourage your girlfriends from leaving the party scene to congregate somewhere else.
- If you're having a sit-down meal, don't assign seats at the table. As much as you want your guests to mix, let them do that on their own. It's okay if all the boys sit on one side of the table and all the girls on the other. They can still talk comfortably.
- Definitely don't plan any activities that are going to embarrass somebody. You might be ready to play coed Twister, but not everybody your age is, especially boys. And be careful about games like truth or

dare, where the pressure is on to reveal secrets. Anything that requires boys and girls to touch or talk about stuff they wouldn't bring up naturally is something you'll want to steer away from. This party is about having a good, comfortable, relaxed time. As the hostess, you can make it so!

The Hostess with the Mostest

Offer hospitality to one another without grumbling. Each one should use whatever gift he has received to serve others, faithfully administering God's grace.

1 Peter 4:9–10

You're ready! The guest list's been made out and the invitations sent. The party food's cooling in the refrigerator. The games are all planned; the prizes are all set. The table, in fact the whole party room, looks smashing, right down to the party favors you made yourself. You have a killer theme, and every single thing about your party is tied to it, including the colors of the Gummy Bears. The doorbell's about to ring, and all you have to do now is *party!*

Right?

Hm ... well ... not quite.

Now is when your real job begins. The minute you open the door to your first guest, you become the **hostess**. That means you're responsible for doing everything you can to make sure each guest has a good time.

Before you freak and call the whole thing off, think about this: Being the hostess of your own party can be a very cool thing. It can make you feel grown up, capable of serving people and making them happy. It's a woman thing—maybe even your first taste of what it's going to be like to someday be the lady of your own house. What a fun way to practice for an important part of womanhood! Besides—it's a God thing.

HOW IS THIS A God Thing?

The instruction to "be a hostess"—or, more clearly, to "be hospitable"—is woven throughout the Bible, right in there with "be righteous," "be holy," and "be joyful."

You trip over verses about it all the time. "Practice hospitality" (Romans 12:13). "Do not forget to entertain strangers, for by doing so some people have entertained angels without knowing it" (Hebrews 13:2). "The overseer must be [among other things] hospitable" (1 Timothy 3:2).

Of course, God isn't talking about just showing your guests where the bathroom is and making sure everybody gets enough bean dip. He's referring to giving food and shelter to the people who are out there spreading the Good News (3 John 5–8). His form of hospitality is some pretty heavy stuff.

And so is yours, in a way. Yes, you're making sure your guests are well taken care of, but your reason for doing it is just like those people's in the New Testament: These are your friends, and you're showing your appreciation for them. As we've chatted about here in *The Best Bash Book,* that's what a party is for. It's a time for celebrating the people in your life and what they mean to you.

That *is* heavy stuff, and it requires some real skills on your part as the hostess. Let's explore what those are.

The Ultimate Hostess

- remembers that the party is not about her but about her guests (unlike when she was little and she was the guest of honor at her own birthday party)
- is ready a half hour before the guests are scheduled to come
- greets every guest as she arrives (she's not back in the bedroom with her best friend agonizing over the fact that her hair makes her look like a poodle)
- is warm and friendly to every guest (including the cousin her mother *made* her invite)
- introduces guests who haven't met before (more on how later), including her parents if they don't know all her guests
- gives them any instructions they need (such as this is where you can put your present or this is where you can hang your coat or this is where you can change into your swimsuit)
- makes sure each person is comfortable (for instance, each person knows where the munchies are if the grazing has begun)
- has something for guests to do when they arrive so they don't stand around feeling awkward (remember the icebreaker activities we talked about in chapter 5?)
- is clear about game instructions and when it's time to move on to the next activity, but isn't bossy about it
- doesn't show favoritism to her best friend the whole time
- tries to include everybody, especially the shyer people
- is relaxed herself, because she's planned everything carefully—and so her guests are relaxed too
- doesn't get upset or sulk if things don't go exactly the way she'd planned
- gets a big kick out of serving people and seeing that they have a good time

- waits until last to be served food
- doesn't make a big deal out of it if somebody spills or breaks something
- stays with the guests until the last one leaves
- thanks every guest for coming

Perhaps you're getting suspicious. "Are you talking about manners here?" you may be shouting at the page. "Isn't this kind of formal? How come I have to worry about all that when nobody else my age does? You should *see* the way some kids behave at parties!"

Whoa! We're not talking about white gloves at the White House here! We're referring to those simple matters of consideration and respect that make the people around you more comfortable, and not only them, but yourself too.

It's My Party and I'll Cry If I Want To

You can memorize the above list and carry it out perfectly—and bummer things may still happen. You're the hostess, and it's up to you to handle them (or recognize them and get help), and you can, even if you're only eight years old. It's all in being prepared.

Girlz WANT TO KNOW

✿   **LILY: I have my party all planned, but I'm so nervous I think I don't want to have it anymore!**

Ah, the old pre-party panic. That happens to almost every hostess, sometimes just as she's opening the door for her first guest. It's like a clear voice in your head saying, "Why am I doing this? What was I thinking?" It's natural to be nervous because you want everybody to have a good time, and as much as you plan and prepare, you can't control whether they do or not. There are a couple of things you can do to soothe those jitters though. First, invite your best friend to come a couple of hours early so you two can get dressed together and she can help keep your mind off every little detail that's driving you nuts. Second, you can tell yourself—because it's true—that once the first couple of people arrive and start having fun, you're going to forget the butterflies in your stomach and start having a good time yourself.

❀ *RENI: I went to this one party where everybody got there, like, all at once, and there was all this noise—and then, all of a sudden, there was a dead silence. The girl who was giving the party looked like she wanted to die. How can I keep that from happening at my party?*

That happens even at adult parties, and the solution is easy: Don't panic. Seriously, it's that simple. Instead of wanting to die because even the biggest mouth in your class is suddenly stricken with terminal shyness, get your icebreaker going. Point people to the snacks. Put on some music. Most of all, start having a good time yourself. Probably all those people with their deadpan expressions were waiting for the hostess to show them how it was done!

❀ *SUZY: How will I know if everybody's having fun?*

There are two ways. First, look at yourself every once in a while. Are you relaxed? Munching on goodies? Enjoying the games and activities? Chances are your guests are too. Second, look around. Are people smiling, laughing, talking, and getting involved in things? If they are, they're fine. People really do want to have fun at parties. Your party isn't a test to see if you can force people to yuk it up against their will!

❀ *ZOOEY: My mom says the party has to be over by 4:30. What if I can't get people to go home? It would be so embarrassing to say, "Okay, time to leave!"*

That would be embarrassing, and fortunately you don't have to do that. Here are some ways to make sure the party's over when it's supposed to be.

- Put what time your party begins and ends on the invitation—2:00 P.M.–4:30 P.M.

- When all the activities are over and the food's been served and it's 4:30, say something like, "Thanks for coming, everybody. I hope you had a good time."
- If nobody makes a move to leave, you can add, "Does anyone need to use the phone to call your parents to come get you?"
- If you have just a few hangers-on, you can look at your watch and say, "Wow, it's five o'clock already. What time does your mom want you home for dinner?" or "I'd love to have you stay longer, but we have plans for the evening."
- With your parents' approval, you can really give a strong hint by saying, "Do you need my mom or dad to drive you home?"
- Try to avoid the point-blank approach: "You better go now before my mom gets mad," or "Didn't you read the invitation? The party's over at 4:30!"
- If all else fails, get your mom or dad to help you. Remember that if somebody doesn't want to go home, that's a compliment to what a great party you threw!

KRESHA: What if something awful happens—like one of my brothers sticks his hand in my cake or there aren't enough prizes or all the balloons and streamers fall down right in the middle of a game? I'd feel so stupid!

But why? Stuff happens! You're there with your friends eating the food you like to eat and doing the things you like to do together. If your brother sticks his hand in the cake, you all laugh about it and cut around that little handprint. If there aren't enough prizes, you grin and hand out IOUs. If the decorations fall down, divide the balloons up among your friends, trash the streamers, and get on with the game. After the party's over, don't remind people about those small catastrophes. In fact, think of them only long enough to figure out what you can learn from them. Don't leave your brother alone with the food. Get more prizes than you think you'll need. Use tacks instead of tape to hang decorations. Don't let your own party scare you. Plan. Prepare. Then have one big-time good time yourself.

✿ *LILY: I know I'm supposed to introduce people that don't know each other, but I don't know the right way. I feel like a geek doing it.*

Here Are Some ANTI-GEEK Instructions

1. Say the name of the person who is older first.

   EXAMPLE: Mom, this is Carrie Jenkins from my gymnastics class. Carrie, this is my mom, Mrs. Robbins.

2. Always use Mr. or Mrs. when introducing adults to kids. The adults can then say whether it's okay to call them by a first name.

   EXAMPLE: Dad, this is Jennifer Daniels. Jennifer, my father, Mr. Robbins.

3. If you're introducing one person who knows no one to a whole crowd whose members all know each other, don't stand in the middle of the room with the new person and say, "Hey, guys, this is Rachel. Rachel, this is everybody." Take Rachel around and introduce her individually to everyone while some activity is going on. Give Rachel some identification tips along with the names too.

   EXAMPLE: Rachel, I want you to meet Joe Higginbotham. Joe, this is Rachel White. Joe's got eight cats at home—can you stand it?

More Hostess Hang-ups

As a hostess, you might have to deal with a couple of other common party problems—perhaps we should call them party *people* who might give you trouble.

The Party Pooper: This is the guest who will hug the wall and refuse to participate no matter what you do. You could bring in a boxful of ten-dollar bills to hand out and she'd still sit there looking and acting as if she were bored out of her skull.

Problem Party Person Solution: Your wallflower guest may look bored, but she's probably shy. Try drawing her in by introducing her to individuals and getting them connected. "You two both like to roller blade. How cool is that?" If that doesn't help, maybe it's because she's supersensitive about her appearance. You may think she looks terrific in those capri pants, but she might have suddenly decided she's a dead ringer for a scarecrow in them and doesn't want to stand up. Try complimenting her on her hair, her nail polish, or her earrings. Be genuine. You can always find something cool to say about every person. If you try those things and she still doesn't want to mix or participate, don't try to force her. Maybe she prefers to just watch for a while. Maybe once she sees everybody else having a blast, she won't be able to help joining in. Or maybe she'll go home still pouting, but it won't be because you didn't try to include her. Pray for her, but don't stress. It isn't your fault.

The Party Animal: This guest is the opposite. She's the one who wants to take over your whole party. Whatever game you announce, the party animal will suggest something else. Whatever music you play, she'll criticize it and offer to call her mom to bring over *her* CD collection. Whatever food you serve, she'll wish out loud that you'd fed her something else. And she's very likely to get rowdy or push the limits. If you've explained that your parents' room is off limits during the treasure hunt, you'll be sure to find her groping under their bed. If you're making ice-cream sundaes, she's a prime candidate for grabbing the whipped-cream can and squirting her fellow guests right there in the dining room. If she gets the least bit bored, she'll be the first one to suggest a game of dodge ball with your mom's knickknacks.

Problem Party Person Solution: First off, don't fight fire with fire. Don't be loud, rowdy, and pushy with *her* to show her whose party it is. Instead, handle each incident quickly and calmly and then move on. When she suggests a party game nobody's ever heard of, tell her you'll try it at *her* next party and go on teaching the game you've planned. When she tries to go home and retrieve her CD collection, assure her she doesn't need to because your music will be fine and then crank up your CD player. When she complains about the food, ask her if she'll pass the chips or keep everybody's glass filled, and keep smiling. When she starts to juggle with your mom's salt-and-pepper shaker collection, ask Mom to walk casually through the party room and see what happens. Do I need to suggest that next time you have a party, leave the party animal off the guest list?

The Party Crasher: It happens sometimes—you're having a sleepover and a bunch of boys find out about it and come around to throw stuff at the window, toilet paper the yard, or try to get guests to sneak out. Or you've taken a bunch of your friends to the skating rink for your birthday and people you don't even know—or particularly like—horn in on the action. Or you're having a backyard pool party and the neighbor kids and their cousins appear at the fence with towels in hand. Some of your other guests may say, "Cool! The more the merrier!" But hey, this is *your* party! You've been planning it for weeks! Yet you don't want to have to act like a bouncer and run people off. What do you do?

Problem Party Person Solution: This is the simplest one yet. This is one of the reasons you *have* parents. Let them deal with it! Seriously, inform your mom or dad (or both) that you have uninvited visitors in the yard or out there in the rink or standing at the gate looking forlorn. Then go back to the guests you did invite. Don't get involved at all. Your parents will handle it wonderfully well. Neither you nor your guests will be embarrassed, and the party will go on as planned. Don't you love it?

The Pushy Parent: On the other hand, sometimes it feels like your parents are the problem! Maybe they hover a little too much over the snack table. Maybe they make too many suggestions when you're playing a game or are involved in some kind of activity. Perhaps they get into conversations with your guests while you're all at the table instead of letting all of you just talk to each other the way you've envisioned it night after night since you started planning this shindig! Or perhaps, worst of all, your folks yell at somebody for running through the house or splashing in the pool or—say it isn't so—yell at *you* in front of your friends! It can be enough to make you want to wrap yourself up in crepe paper and die.

Problem Party Person Solution: The answer to this dilemma is in knowing your own parents and thinking way beforehand about how they might act during your party. Then be what's called *proactive*. That means head the problem off before it ever occurs. Does your mom usually hover around you and your friends, insisting that you keep your bedroom door open when you're in there talking, constantly asking if everyone has sunscreen or needs to use a restroom? Talk to her before the party and ask her if you can be the hostess this time and take care of your friends yourself. You don't need to remind her that she's smothering you. Just focus on what you would like to do. Ask her if she'll help you by doing the behind-the-scenes stuff, like refilling the chips basket.

Does your dad usually ask your friends so many questions they feel like they're on a witness stand? Ask him to do a job during the party that will keep him too busy to cross-examine—like videotape the whole thing or play soda-fountain man or keep an eye out for that group of boys you know is going to try to crash your bash.

Do your parents tend to discipline you in public or scold your friends the same way they do you? Sit down with them before the party and come up with a list of guidelines they'd like your guests to follow. Then find a fun way to let your guests know what they are—maybe some clever signs posted around the pool or a passing comment like, "You can make anything you want with these craft supplies except a mess!"

If your parents do embarrass you in some way during your party, try not to make a big deal of it at the time. Grin, bear it, and go on with the festivities. Later, maybe while you're cleaning up and thanking them for letting you have the party, you could say something like, "Next time, Dad, could you maybe not ask my friends quite so many questions? I don't think they talk as much about stuff like that at their houses." Don't whine or pout though. That'll get you nowhere, and they may be reluctant to let you have another party.

The Party's Over

By the time the last guest leaves, you're going to be pretty pooped. It takes a lot of energy to throw a party. You can head for the nearest beanbag chair, right?

Not yet! There are a couple more things you're responsible for before you go to your room and relive the whole thing in your daydreams. The good hostess always **cleans up** and **follows up.**

Cleanup: Unless you have a paid cleaning staff at your house (you wish!), you're responsible for at least helping until the house is returned to its original state—a good thing to think about when you're transforming the whole place into a bowling alley or something! Here are some ways to make it easier on you and your mom and dad.

- Throughout the party, whenever you see stuff lying around and everybody else is involved in something, do a little pickup. Toss those used paper plates and napkins into a garbage bag. Scoop up those broken pieces of pretzel from the rug. Dump the remains of that abandoned Coke in the sink. That doesn't mean run around fussing over things the entire time. Just be aware of any little messes you can clean up along the way.
- If you're having stand-up snacks or an outside meal, make big trash cans available for pitching stuff, and your guests will do it themselves. If you're serving sodas in cans or bottles, be sure you have special recycling containers available.
- Ask brothers and sisters who want to be involved in your party if they'll keep things picked up during the event. You can reward them by letting them play one of the games or having one of the favors or promising them you'll do something with them later, like make Playdough or watch some maddening kid-video with them (you have to make it worth their while).
- Ask your best friend to stay after and help you clean up. She could later have pizza with you and your family or spend the night and review the party with you into the wee hours of the morning!
- Be aware of all there is to do. This might include washing dishes, putting food away, taking decorations down, rearranging the furniture,

mopping up spills, vacuuming crumbs, and tossing trash. Don't collapse until it's all done. Hang in there with Mom and Dad until the bitter end!

Follow-Up: Shortly after your party is over—within the next day—be sure you do these things.

- Thank your parents for letting you have the party. Be specific about how great they were. Did your mom go all out with the cupcakes? Did you dad build a puppet theater? Did they both handle that kid beautifully—the one who tried to play Tarzan from the chandelier? Thank them with everything you've got.
- Tell your siblings you appreciate what they did—even if it was staying out of the way or keeping the dog under control.
- Show your appreciation to friends who helped you, whether with decorations, invitations, food, or keeping you from crying when some girl said your games were dumb.
- Write thank-you notes to people who brought you presents. You might think, "Oh, come on! This isn't my Great-Aunt Daisy! This is my best friend. I see her every day! Why do I have to write to her?" Well, think about it. Didn't your best friend—or anybody else—have to find a time to shop for your present, pick out something just right for you, spend her own money or her mom's, and wrap it? That's a lot of time and effort, and it deserves to be recognized by a little time and effort from you. It doesn't have to be anything long and fancy, but it should be something that comes from your heart. Here's an example:

Dear Reni,
I can't believe you got me that scrapbook for my birthday!
I've been wanting that for so long, and when I opened the package, I just about freaked. I can't wait to start filling it up. You could even help me do some of the pages. You're the best friend ever.
Love,
Lily

Notice that Lily doesn't say, "Dear Reni, thanks for the present. I like it." She names the specific gift and makes a comment about it, and of course, puts a little of her own personality in there. Reni will be jazzed to get that in the mail. Wouldn't you be?

- Thank God for helping you do such a good job. He's up there grinning because you're learning about hospitality.
- Now you can bask in the afterglow! Why not even make a little scrap-book of your party, with a copy of the invitation, the guest list, some decoration scraps, and photos if any were taken? You can even write some captions on each page to capture the fun stuff you might not remember later if you don't get them down on paper. This was a big deal. Stretch the joy out as long as you can!

That's it. Here in *The Best Bash Book*, we've covered all the things that are involved in throwing a party. Now that you know all this stuff, how do you feel at this point about the whole party thing? Let's check you out.

Put an exclamation point (!) next to each statement that you can honestly say right now:

_____Planning a party sounds like a blast.

_____I already have an idea for a theme.

_____I know what kind of party I'd like to have.

_____I bet I can make a party happen even if my parents don't have a lot of money to spend on it.

_____I know people I could invite to a party.

_____Invitations are no problem!

_____I like to think about what kind of food I'd have at my party.

_____I have so many ideas for games and other stuff to do, I'll probably have trouble choosing which ones to actually do.

_____I can just picture the party room all decorated.

_____I can imagine myself being the hostess.

_____Problem Party People? I've got that handled!

Count up your exclamation marks and put the number you have here: _____

If you have 8 or more !'s, you're definitely ready to throw a party! Your mind is teeming with ideas, and you can hardly sit still for thinking about the whole thing. So have a ball! Plan to your little heart's content. Don't forget about including Mom in the plans though, and be ready to lop a few ideas off the agenda so your gig doesn't get out of control. You'll still have a blast getting it all together, because you, girl, are ready to party!

If you have between 4 and 7 !'s, the idea of having a party intrigues you, but there are still some doubts in your mind. That doesn't mean you shouldn't still throw one. It just means you'll want to review the chapters that are about the things you didn't mark *and* it means you might need a lot of help from Mom along the way. There's nothing wrong with that. If the two of you plan carefully, it'll be great. Enjoy!

If you had 3 or fewer !'s, not to worry. You're a little party-shy. It's okay if you're not quite ready to make up a guest list and send out invitations. Wait a little while as the idea grows on you. If you really would like to have a party but you're worried about a lot of the things on the list, start small. Have three friends over for a tea party, or invite several girls in for an hour of Valentine making and heart-shaped cookies. You can still go through all the steps, and once you get the hang of the process, you'll be ready for a bigger bash. Even if you want to daydream about a party for another year, that's okay too. Parties aren't a requirement for growing up—they're just one of the fun parts! But they aren't fun unless you're ready, so give yourself plenty of time to get there.

Talking to God About It

Dear _____, *(your favorite way of addressing God)*
I now know all the basic stuff for having a party, and I'm feeling
_____ *about it. I know you'll help me when it*
comes to _____.
    *Most of all though, I'm counting on you to help me with **responsibility**. This hostess thing is big stuff, and I want to do it right. Will you help me to be responsible about all the things I've checked off here?*

_____ sharing all my hopes and plans with my parents
_____ accepting their final word

_____taking people's feelings into consideration when I do my inviting

_____not getting carried away with food and decorations

_____picking activities I know people will enjoy

_____giving my party for the right reason—which is not to show every-body else up!

_____being a good hostess

_____helping with clean-up

_____remembering to thank everybody

I know I won't be perfect, God, but I also know I'll be a whole bunch better at all of this if I stay close to you and do things the way you want me to do them. Please help me do that, okay? You're the best. Amen.

_____ *(your name)*

Once at a party, I saw the hostess come to the rescue. Here's what happened:

Special Party Feature: THE ULTIMATE FIELD-TRIP PARTY

It Looks Like This: This is a party you want to take on the road (outside to some really cool park or the beach or up a trail for a hike and picnic) or to a restaurant-type place that has space for parties (anything from McDonald's to a Japanese hibachi grill) or to an attraction or event (a great movie, a museum, a theme park, or a chocolate factory). These parties are often easier on busy parents who don't have time to help you plan and put things together, and they're usually a sure way to delight your guests. Their only drawbacks are the expense and responsibility for moms and dads of having other people's kids in a public place.

This Much Space: For an outside party, you need plenty of room for your number of guests to run around—or why be outside, right? But you'll still want to have boundaries so you and your parents can keep track of everybody. "The whole beach" doesn't work as well as "from here to the pier." If you're having your field-trip party at an eating establishment, the folks there will tell you how many people they can accommodate in their party space. Be sure you have a room that is yours alone; restaurant parties that are open to traffic of other customers aren't usually as much fun—too many distractions.

Guest List: It's best to limit your guest list for this kind of party for a couple of reasons. One is the cost. If you take the festivities to the movies and then to an ice-cream parlor, you're talking at least eight to ten dollars a person. You do the math—that mounts up. And since you're inviting people to join you in your celebration, it isn't polite to ask your guests to pay their own way. The other reason to keep the invitations to a minimum is the number of people your mom and dad can keep track of at Six Flags or the roller rink or the back room at Fuddrucker's. Unless they want to invite other chaperones along—and pay their way too—you shouldn't have more than ten people, including you. If you're thinking of something like horseback riding or a tour of the local television station, find out how many people they can handle at one time. (Your mom will also want to know if she has to pay in advance and if there is a refund for guests who don't show.)

Inviting Ideas: Your invitations can be fun because it will be easy to match them up with the event you have planned. Going to an Italian place for the best pizza in town? Make invitations that look like slices of pizza. Taking the whole gang to the beach? Send each friend a seashell with the invitation on a tag attached to it. Going on a field trip to the aquarium? Make paper starfish. Once you've designed your invitations, be sure to include all the important information— whether you're all meeting at your house or at the party scene; how to get to the park or restaurant or whatever if they're to meet you there; what you're paying for and whether they might need spending money for additional treats; what clothes or other equipment they'll need (like sunscreen), and what time they should be picked up when the party's over and where.

Food for Thought: Unless you're centering your party around a restaurant, the food isn't as important at a field trip as at other kinds of get-togethers, but your guests will still want to eat. The beauty of a Burger King Birthday or Baskin Robbins Bash is that you don't have to worry about the food—and if cooking isn't your or your mom's thing, this can be good! Tell the restaurant folks how many people will be there and find out exactly what they'll provide. Have your mom talk to the other moms about any food allergies your guests may have so she can take care of that. Just as at an at-home party, this isn't the time to introduce your friends to some exotic food they may never have had before, like lobster, caviar, or squid. If your field trip is centered on something else, like a play, a tour, or water sports, the food is there to fill tummies and help everybody refuel. Keep it simple, especially since it will have to be transported. Remember that pizza places will deliver to parks! One word of caution: If your entire party time is outside, be sure to have plenty of water and other drinks on hand. Nothing wilts a celebration like thirsty people with no fluids.

Stuff to Do: That's a piece of cake if you're going out for burgers and video games or an afternoon movie and ice-cream sundaes. If you're holding your party at a park or the beach, there will be plenty to do already, but it's a good idea to have a couple of organized games ready to roll in case people get restless. It's even helpful to have a play-while-you-eat word game prepared if you're having lunch in the party room at a restaurant. It keeps the conversation going and everybody focused (including that one girl who is sure to start a mashed potato fight if she gets the least bit bored).

Dressing It Up: You definitely won't *have* to do any decorating, but there are a couple of exceptions if you *want* to dress up your party. If the whole group is meeting at your house before taking off for the party site, it's fun to make a cool sign for the front door. If you're having food in a pavilion at the park, balloons and streamers or other decorations aren't out of the question if it's not too windy. If a restaurant is your destination, find out if you can decorate the party room and when. Even if the group is meeting someplace else, like the entrance to the zoo, you can tie a bunch of balloons to the fence to make the spot more visible.

Caution:

- If your mom or dad is driving the guests, be sure you have plenty of room and that everybody will have a seat belt. It's okay to ask another mom to drive too—as long as you buy her a burger or a movie ticket as well.
- For the park or beach, take food that won't spoil. Avoid things made with mayo. It might be good to take sandwich fixings with you and make the sandwiches there so the bread doesn't get soggy.
- If you have a car ride longer than ten minutes, plan some car games to keep everybody from getting bored.
- Check out where the bathrooms are so you can tell your guests when they arrive—especially for an outdoor party.
- Tell everyone where to meet if they get separated from the group, especially if you're going to a theme park or zoo where the group will be moving around.
- If your party is to be held in a restaurant or park pavilion, reservations will have to be made several weeks ahead of time. Then have your

mom or dad call a few days before the party to confirm the reservation. Wouldn't it be a bummer to show up and find somebody else having a party in your space?

- If you're going to the movies, have an adult go ahead of time and buy the tickets so you can hand them out when your guests arrive.
- Have a back-up plan for an outdoor party in case the weather turns bad. An indoor picnic can be a blast—spread a blanket on the floor and turn on some nature music! Volleyball in the basement can work. Board games on your screen porch can be—well—different! Just be sure to contact your guests when the thunder starts rolling to let them know the party's still on with a slight change of plans. And don't be too bummed. Remember that the whole point of the party is to get together with friends and enjoy each other, no matter where you are.

Be My Guest!

"When you enter a house, first say, 'Peace to this house.' ... Stay in that house, eating and drinking whatever they give you."

Luke 10:5–7

When It's Somebody Else's Party

As much fun as it is to plan your own party, it's sometimes even more of a blast to go to a party somebody *else* is giving. You can relax and enjoy all the food, games, and decorations your hostess and her mom have put together. It's a celebration of you, one of her friends. How cool!

In the gospel of Luke 14:7–11, Jesus talked about not taking the place of honor at a table where you're a guest but rather waiting for the host to tell you where to sit. He was showing us what kind of persons God wants us to be. Good manners are one way we can let other people know that we respect them.

You could probably use a little of that kind of advice right now as you face a lot of new stuff in your life. You're doing a bunch of things you didn't get to do when you were younger, like go to sleepovers, go on field trips, and attend parties at school and at other people's houses without your parents there. You might be a little anxious as you think about some of those things. Will you know where the bathroom is? What if they serve food you don't like? What do you do around people you don't know? And just as it's important for you to do the correct and considerate things when you're the party-*giver,* it's good to do those same kinds of things when you're the party-*goer.* Yes, your hostess wants you to kick back, but there are guest manners you'll want to know about. Wouldn't you know that it would be a God thing?

HOW IS THIS A God Thing?

That's pretty easily answered. Remember the second great commandment Jesus gave out? He said, "Love your neighbor as yourself." He meant for you to treat the people around you with the same consideration you want them to use with you. That's all manners are—at a party or anywhere.

Manners are guidelines for you to follow so you don't feel uncomfortable in new situations. If you follow the rules, you won't be embarrassed, and you'll even help the people around you to feel more comfortable. After all, not every

parent is teaching manners these days, so by setting a good example, you're being sort of a mini-mom.

Besides, people do form their opinions of you by the way you behave. When you're chewing with your mouth open and yakking away the entire time, people will think you're pretty sloppy. When you shove your way to the head of the food line, people will get the idea you're rude and greedy. When you shout, "Hey, don't you have any Pepsi? I don't drink Coke!" people will scratch you off their guest list!

God wants us to show respect and kindness to others. Manners give us instructions for doing that, that's all. You won't appear stiff and stuffy. In fact, other kids will start doing what you're doing because you look so at ease.

CHECK Yourself OUT

Let's see how much you already know about the manners a party guest should use. Decide whether each statement below is true or false and write T or F in the little space.

_____ 1. Being on time is no big deal. This is a party, not school!

_____ 2. When the hostess opens the door, wait until you're invited in before you go inside the house.

_____ 3. If somebody isn't already introducing you to people you don't know, go ahead and introduce yourself.

_____ 4. If you don't like the food, say so. It's always best to be honest.

_____ 5. You don't need to try a game if it sounds dumb to you.

_____ 6. If you think the decorations are kind of lame, it's better not to comment on them at all.

_____ 7. If you don't see a party favor or goody bag, it's okay to go ahead and ask where it is.

_____ 8. When you leave, make sure you say good-bye to the hostess and tell her you had a good time.

_____ 9. There is no need to say good-bye to the girl's parents; after all, it's her party.

_____ 10. If it's time for the party to be over but you're still having a good time, it's okay to hang out as long as you want to.

_____ 11. If you have to leave early, make an announcement about it to the whole group so they'll know why you're going before the party's over.

Let's see how you did. Remember, if you put an F when it should have been a T or a T when an F was the right answer, that doesn't mean you're a Manners Dummy. It simply means you just learned something new.

1. **False.** It's not polite to be late. If you get to a party fifteen minutes after it was supposed to begin, the whole group might be waiting for you to start the first game, sit down to lunch, or leave for the movie theater. Bad form!

2. **True.** In any situation when you go to someone else's home, it's always polite to wait until you're invited in, even after the door is opened. No shoving past the hostess to get to the refreshment table!

3. **True.** Do introduce yourself. Nothing is more awkward than standing around with a bunch of people whose names you don't know. You'll make everybody feel more comfortable if you simply say something like, "Hi, I'm Lily. Are you a friend of Reni's too?"

4. **False.** If you don't like the food, keep that to yourself. After all, somebody went to a lot of trouble to prepare it, so to say, "Ugh, this is nasty. Could I have something else?" is sure to hurt somebody's feelings (and get you on the "Don't Invite Her Back" list). Instead, nibble at it a little and then quietly put your paper plate in the trash can or set your dish aside. If somebody says, "You didn't like the quiche?" it's fine to say, "I wasn't very hungry. It sure looks good though."

5. **False.** Don't assume a game isn't going to be fun just because it _sounds_ "dumb." Give every activity your best shot. You might be surprised and find out it's a blast. If it really is a lame game, it won't last that long anyway. Remember that a party is about celebrating being together. You can make any game fun if it's being played with people you like. We'll talk later in this

chapter about what to do if you think a game is not appropriate or you're sure your parents wouldn't want you to play it.

6. *True!* You've probably figured out by now that it's important not to
hurt the hostess' feelings. You also know after reading this
book how much energy, time, and imagination it takes to put a
party together. Even if you don't like the decorations—or the
food or the games or the color of the napkins—you can appreciate the effort behind them. In fact, you can even say, "Wow,
Zooey—you sure put a lot of time into this party!" You'll still
be telling the truth, and she'll be pleased at the compliment.

7. *False!* A party hostess isn't required to give out favors or goody
bags! Those are supposed to be gifts for the guests. Do you sit
down at your own birthday party and say, "Okay, where are
my presents?" If goodies for the guests do appear, show your
appreciation. If they don't, show your manners by saying
nothing at all.

8. *True!* It's pretty rude to leave a party without saying good-bye to
your hostess. Making a positive comment about the party is a
good idea too—something like, "That was great, Suzy. Could
your mom give my mom the recipe for those cookies? I could
live off those!" or "I
had a good time,
Kresha. Those
were cool games."

9. *False!* Since you know by
now that no girl
your age does a party
by herself, it's really
good manners to
say good-bye to
your hostess'
mom too and
thank her for
everything.

10. **False.** Check your invitation before you go to the party to find out what time it's supposed to be over. Arrange to have someone pick you up at that time. It's okay to extend your stay at the hostess' house only if both she and her mom invite you—without your asking! As delightful a guest as you are, they're both still going to need some rest after the festivities. Don't worry, if you've been considerate, you'll be invited back.

11. **False.** If you have to leave early, take your hostess and her mom aside and tell them when you arrive. Then when it's time to go, slip out as quietly as you can. That way, you don't take the focus away from the party and put it on yourself.

Polish!

Those are your basic party manners. Once you've got those down—and they aren't hard when you're concentrating on other people's feelings—you can begin to polish your etiquette for social gatherings. Here's how to get that wonderful party shine!

RSVP

At the bottom of the invitation you've received, you may see the four letters RSVP. As we talked about in chapter 3, in French they stand for, "Answer, if you please." The hostess wants to know if you'll be coming so she can plan food, favors, games, how many chairs to have at the table, and all that stuff. Give her a call at home. It's better not to discuss the party at school in case someone who wasn't invited overhears and gets her feelings hurt. (Do you see a theme being repeated here?)

When you were a little kid, your mom probably did the RSVP'ing for you, but now that you're older and more mature, it's time to take that responsibility for yourself. If you want to have some fun with it, you can write your response and send it, doing it in the same style as the invitation. If you were invited to an Easter egg hunt, for instance, and the invitation had a bunny with a basket of eggs on the front, draw and color an Easter egg and write, "I'll be there with my basket" on it and pop it into an envelope and drop it into the mail.

Make Your Mom Happy

Get as much information about the party as you can if it isn't on the invitation. Your mom will want to know stuff like whether dinner's going to be served or you should eat first, if you're supposed to take a present, what time you should be picked up, and whether you'll need money for the video arcade. Don't tell your mom she's worrying too much or hint that she ought to call the hostess' mom herself. It's all about the responsibility thing, girlfriend.

Dress the Part

When you were way little, your mom probably picked out your dress and lacy socks for the birthday parties you went to. When you got a little older, it didn't matter that much because you were bound to get chocolate frosting down the front of whatever you wore. But now that you're maturing, wearing the appropriate thing is not only fun but also helps you feel more comfortable at parties. Ever show up at a birthday party wearing your Easter dress only to find everybody else in T-shirts and Nikes? It can make you feel out of place. Here are some hints for dressing for the parties you go to.

- Look at what kind of party it is and that will narrow things down. You'll obviously wear something different to a clambake on the beach than to a reception after somebody's piano recital.
- If it's a "regular" party—you're going to Burger King and then to the movies or you're spending the night in the attic with five other girls— ask the hostess what she's going to wear.
- Knowing what the general category of dress is—grungy, casual, dressy, or formal—you can then fit in your own style. If the hostess says it's going to be a dressy tea and you feel like a sore toe in a dress, wear a nice pair of pants and a pretty blouse. Leave the clunky tennis shoes at home. If she tells you it's a casual backyard barbecue and you were counting on dressing to the max, put on a cute sundress and some

matching sandals (and take shorts and a top along in case you decide you want to help build sand castles in their giant sandbox after all).

Have Fun!

We've said over and over here in *The Best Bash Book* that the whole purpose of giving a party is to show your friends a good time. When you go to a party, your purpose is to have a good time. The hostess has done her part, so now you'll need to do yours. "Have fun" sounds like easy directions, but if you're a little nervous about what to do and how to act at parties, that can be a tall order. Here are some tips that might help you relax a little.

- Worrying about what the other people at the party are thinking of you? That's called being self-conscious, and it's the surest way to ruin your good time! Instead, concentrate on what those people are like and on the games and food, and soon you'll realize you aren't self-conscious anymore. You're just being you.
- A little freaked out about what to do when you first get there? Ask your closest friend who's going if you can ride with her or give her a ride so the two of you arrive together. That can help you feel more comfortable. Don't plan to stick to her like one strip of Velcro to another the entire time, or you'll miss out on the other cool people at the party. But do think of it as a good way to break the I-just-got-here tension you might feel.
- Sure you aren't going to know anybody and will feel like a loser because no one talks to you? Look around at the party for somebody else who looks as if she's a little lost and go over and introduce yourself to her. You know how grateful you would feel if someone else did that for you, so do it for her. It's a definite God thing.
- Still too shy to talk to people right away? Then enjoy looking at the decorations, checking out the food table, and watching people as they arrive, while you get your bearings. If the hostess is the only one you know, don't try to get her into a conversation in the corner. She has to attend to all of her guests. Besides, she probably invited you because she wants you to know her other friends, so go for it.

- Afraid you'll be terrible at the games? Let's think about this—it isn't physical education class at school! Nobody's going to give you a grade or yell at you if you look spastic. Games are for fun. There's no "great" or "terrible." Join in. Laugh at your mistakes. If a game or activity is being done that you truly feel uncomfortable doing, it's okay to say, "I think I'll sit this one out." But don't pout on the sidelines. Watch and cheer the other players on. The last thing you want is for your hostess to feel as if she's done something wrong. (If you really feel she's way out of line—perhaps encouraging a kissing game at a boy-girl party— take her aside later and tell her how you feel. For now, just don't participate and don't make a scene. She'll appreciate it and maybe even listen more if you wait until after the party.)

Those Little Prickly Problems ...
Girlz WANT TO KNOW

✿ *LILY: Sometimes I go to parties where everybody in the world has been invited—and I don't always get along with everybody in the world. Is it okay to hang with my own friends at those parties?*

Yes, and then again, no. If it's a sit-around-and-talk or everybody-swim-in-the-pool kind of party, it's fine to just enjoy your own friends, as long as you don't cut yourself off from the chance to meet new people and you don't let somebody you don't know sit off by herself with nobody to be with. If activities are planned and you're divided into teams by the hostess, go with it the best you can. Don't drag her into the bathroom and try to persuade her to rearrange everything so you can be with your best buds and don't have to be with that kid who gives you dirty looks in the library. Don't put her in that position. Be a good sport and see how it turns out. You might be surprised how a change in scene can make for a whole different relationship with a classroom bully or playground snob.

✿ *RENI: I love to play games at parties, but I hate to lose. Even my best friend tells me I take it all too seriously. But aren't you supposed to play to win?*

You play on your bobby sox softball team to win. You play party games to have a good time. Try to forget about winning and losing—just enjoy yourself. Tell yourself beforehand that if you win, you're going to give the prize to somebody else. Concentrate on cheering other people on. You might not see a change in yourself right away, and that's okay. Sometimes it serves you well to be competitive—just not at somebody's birthday celebration! But keep practicing. After a while, it will start to come more naturally to you. Trust me—you're going to have a lot more fun.

❀ *ZOOEY: I love to go to parties, but some of my friends told me after the last one that we went to that I was too loud and rowdy. But it isn't school! I thought I was there to have a good time!*

You are there to have a good time, but if you trust your friends' judgment and you like the way they behave at parties, it wouldn't be a bad idea to consider what they have to say. Do they say you talk a lot and don't give other people a chance to say anything? It's definitely better to give everybody a turn to get her two cents in. Do they tell you that you get carried away and throw food? Your friend's dining room may not be the school cafeteria, but it isn't a monkey cage, either. Bad table manners are never okay! Do they hint that you run through people's homes, knocking things over, or that you put your feet on the furniture and generally don't show respect for your hostess' belongings? Unless you're outside, running is not a good idea. Just because it's a party doesn't mean anything goes. You can still have fun while attempting not to destroy property! Look carefully at your party actions. You sure wouldn't want to be left at home, uninvited, while the rest of your friends continue to go to parties, right?

❀ *SUZY: I get really nervous when I'm invited to a birthday party, because I know the girl's going to open my present in front of everybody. What if she doesn't like it or somebody says something mean about it?*

That definitely shows how important manners are, doesn't it? But since we're talking about you as the giver, think about these ways to avoid being embarrassed. First, ask the birthday girl what she'd like to have. If she tells you she collects something or is really into a certain sport or trend, that will help you choose. Second, ask somebody who is close to her what she's getting for her. Nobody can hit it right on the head like a best friend. Third, if the hostess shows disappointment when she opens her gift, ask her later when you're alone if there is something else she would rather have and encourage her to exchange it. Smile when you tell her where you bought it and assure her that it won't hurt your feelings if she takes it back and gets something else. After all, this is a gift that's supposed to make her happy. Fourth, if other guests make mean remarks about the gift you've brought, ignore them. Sure it hurts, but they obviously haven't read *The Best Bash Book* and don't know any better. Buy them each a copy for when their birthdays come around. Don't run off crying, though, and don't launch into a lecture on their rudeness. Your hostess won't appreciate it.

Talking to God About It

Dear _____, (your favorite way of addressing God)

I think it's cool that I get to go to more and more parties as I get older. I really want to have fun, and I also want to behave in a way that will make you proud. Some of the stuff I've just read about I never heard of before. Could you help me with those things, especially _____? Please help them to come to my mind when I need them. Other stuff I already knew about, but I don't always follow, especially when it comes to _____. Would you help me there? And at those times when as a guest, or a would-be guest, I get my feelings hurt, would you help me to focus on other people instead of always on what I want, especially when _____?

I want to be a gracious party guest so that when I finally come to your house with many rooms, you will welcome me. I love you.

Party on,

_____ (your name)

Lily Pad

I dream of being invited to a party where . . .

The Ultimate Party Planning Sheet

1. Decide exactly what kind of party you're going to have:

2. Decide on a date, a time, and a place:

3. Discuss with your parents how many people you can invite and make up your guest list:

_____   _____

_____   _____

_____   _____

_____   _____

_____   _____

_____   _____

4. Decide what you want your invitations to look like and whether you want to make or buy them:

5. Plan the decorations for the party:

Here's space for doodling ideas:

Plan the food:

Think of what things you'll do at your party—games, activities, entertainment, etc.

Icebreaker to Get the Party Started: (Include the name of the game, stuff you'll need, how it works, prizes, and how it fits your theme.)

Active Games:

Quiet Games:

Decide whether you'll give prizes for game winners and/or favors to everybody:

Go through your plan with your mom and make a shopping list for nonfood items. Include what you'll need for:

invitations

mailing

decorations

games and activities

prizes

- Go shopping for those items so you can get started making them.
- With your mom, make a shopping list for food.
- Go shopping for food closer to party time.
- Arrange a time to help get the party area ready.
- Contact anyone who hasn't RSVP'd.

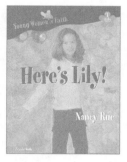
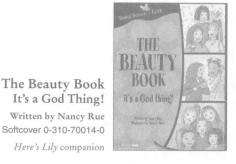

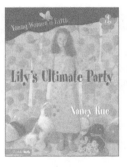
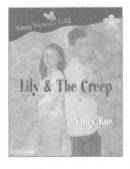
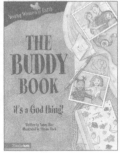

NIV Young Women of Faith Bible
GENERAL EDITOR SUSIE SHELLENBERGER

Designed just for girls ages 8-12, the *NIV Young Women of Faith Bible* not only has a trendy, cool look, it's packed with fun to read in-text features that spark interest, provide insight, highlight key foundational portions of Scripture, and more. Discover how to apply God's word to your everyday life with the *NIV Young Women of Faith Bible*.

Hardcover 0-310-91394-2
Softcover 0-310-70278-X

Available soon at your local bookstore!

Zonder**kidz**™

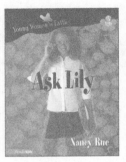